CW01512619

Original title:
Knobby Stems Inside the Phoenix Nub

Author: Eliora Lumiste
ISBN HARDBACK: 978-1-80562-525-4
ISBN PAPERBACK: 978-1-80564-046-2

The Hidden Garden Within the Blaze

In a forest deep, where shadows dance,
Whispers of magic weave their trance.
Flowers bloom in colors bright,
Guarded by the soft moonlight.

A secret path that no one knows,
Where the wild wind in silence blows.
Leaves that shimmer, secrets shared,
A timeless realm, forever spared.

Within the blaze, a garden grows,
With hidden wonders, love bestows.
Roots entwined in ancient lore,
It calls to hearts, an open door.

Creatures pause, with hues so rare,
Dancing lightly in the air.
The scent of dreams on breezes flow,
Carrying tales of long ago.

So venture forth, let spirit soar,
To find the garden and explore.
For in the blaze, beyond the fate,
Lies magic's heart, the hidden gate.

Twisted Growth from Ashen Roots

Beneath the charred and battered ground,
New shoots of life begin to sound.
From ashes soft, a tale unfolds,
Of strength and grace in embers bold.

In twisted forms, the branches curl,
A silent dance, the winds unfurl.
Resilience blooms where shadows lay,
In darkened nights, a brightened day.

Each leaf a whisper, secrets shared,
Of battles fought, of fates declared.
From all that's lost, a new emerges,
In cycles deep, the spirit surges.

Roots grasp the earth with fervent might,
While stars above shine through the night.
Together woven, life's sweet thread,
In every heartbeat, hope is fed.

Thus twisted growth from ash does rise,
Beneath the weight of troubled skies.
From broken pasts, new futures bloom,
In every heart, dispelling gloom.

The Hidden Artistry of Fire

Dancing flames in twilight seen,
With flickering grace, a fiery sheen.
They sculpt the night with vivid light,
A secret art that ignites delight.

Each ember spins a tale unique,
Of warmth and woe, of whispers meek.
The shadows play, the stories flow,
In fiery hues, our dreams we stow.

A canvas bright for spirits bold,
In molten colors, stories told.
Fire's embrace, both fierce and kind,
Ignites the spark within the mind.

Flickers dance to unseen tunes,
Beneath the gaze of watchful moons.
In every crackle, fate entwined,
The artistry of fire, divined.

So let it blaze, this truth we hold,
As life's own flame, a sight so bold.
In hidden depths, the heart concedes,
The artistry in burning deeds.

Stems of Transformation

From roots so deep, the journey starts,
With whispers soft and hopeful hearts.
Each tendril sways, a silent plea,
For change beneath the surface sea.

With every storm that bends and breaks,
A stronger stem, the courage wakes.
In gentle rains, there's growth anew,
From dormant dreams, our spirits grew.

In colors bold, the flowers bloom,
Transforming fears, escaping gloom.
The world awakens, vibrant, bright,
A dance of life, bathed in light.

To shed the past, a graceful fall,
Embracing chance, we heed the call.
In every twist, a tale we write,
In stems of change, we find our might.

Thus rise we up, from dark to day,
As hope takes root, we find our way.
Embracing all, the shifts we face,
In transformation, we find grace.

Within the Fire's Embrace

Within the fire, secrets gleam,
Its glow a whisper, a tender dream.
Warmth envelops, shadows sway,
In flickered moments, night turns day.

The flames caress with tender hands,
Forging bonds, like ancient brands.
In every spark, a promise kept,
The heart's own hush, where silence wept.

Echoes dance in fervent light,
Transforming dark into delight.
As flames entwine with hopes unchained,
In furnace deep, true courage gained.

Through trials fierce, the heart ignites,
Within the fire, we claim our rights.
The heat, a guide through tempest tall,
In flame's embrace, we stand, not fall.

For in the blaze, our spirits soar,
An ardent force, forevermore.
So let the fire burn so bright,
In its embrace, we find our light.

Cracks of Hope in the Scorched Earth

In whispered winds, the stories flow,
Of roots that reach where embers glow.
Through seams of ash, new life will creep,
In cracks of hope, the earth will weep.

With every scar, a tale is spun,
As weary skies meet the morning sun.
Nature's heart beats strong and steady,
In every crevice, hope's already.

From barren ground, green sprouts will rise,
As life insists on claiming skies.
With tendrils grasping wide and slow,
From cracks of hope, new dreams will grow.

The phoenix calls, in flames we trust,
From ashes forged, a bond is just.
Each brittle shard, a thread entwined,
In fractured earth, new strength we find.

Nature's Resilience in the Phoenix Glow

The sun dips low, with fiery grace,
While shadows dance, in dusk's embrace.
From charred remains, the dreams ascend,
In nature's heart, the wounds will mend.

Through fiery trials, tendrils twist,
In every struggle, there's a tryst.
Resilience blooms in colors bright,
As night surrenders to the light.

In every crack, the wild will sprout,
As life persists, a joyful shout.
With every breath, the earth will sing,
In phoenix glow, new hopes take wing.

From darkness birthed, a vibrant hue,
The phoenix waits with dawn anew.
In nature's grace, we find the flow,
Of life restored in radiant glow.

Sinuous Paths Beneath the Flames

Beneath the flames, a river flows,
Through twisted paths where wild winds blow.
In shadowed arcs, the journey winds,
With whispered secrets the forest finds.

The crackling fire, a fierce ballet,
As sprites of ember dance and sway.
Yet underneath, a story brews,
In every twist, fresh strength renews.

Through charred remains, a pathway gleams,
In twisted roots, lie buried dreams.
With every turn, the heart beats true,
In sinuous paths, the world is new.

So let us tread with gentle care,
In the dance of life, a woven dare.
For beneath the flames, life knows no end,
In every curve, a new hope sends.

The Texture of Regeneration

In every scar, a tale unfurls,
Where time reshapes, and magic swirls.
The texture of life, both rough and smooth,
In every line, the heart will soothe.

With gentle rain, the earth will sigh,
As seeds of promise learn to fly.
In whispers soft, the grass will bend,
While shadows fade, and dreams ascend.

The canvas vast, with colors bright,
Each stroke a statement, bold and light.
Regeneration's art displayed,
In every hue, life's serenade.

As seasons shift and time flows free,
The texture of love, infinity.
In every cycle, a story spun,
Of regeneration, a life begun.

Whispering Shoots of Hope

In shadows deep, where whispers dwell,
Soft shoots emerge, their stories tell.
With gentle grace, they greet the light,
A dance of hope, in the calm of night.

Through tendrils green, the world does change,
Each fragile stem, both bold and strange.
They rise anew, from earth's embrace,
A promise held, in time and space.

The sky above, a canvas clear,
Each droplet falls, a song we hear.
With every breath, the heart will sing,
Of future blooms, and what they bring.

In silent whispers, the dreams take flight,
Though storms may brew, they seek the light.
With every heart, a spark ignites,
And whispers grow to mighty heights.

The quiet strength of roots so dear,
In tangled earth, they persevere.
From every fall, they rise again,
In gentle nudges, they learn to mend.

Growth from the Heart of Fire

In ember's glow, a tale unfolds,
Where warmth does rise, and courage molds.
From ashes low, a phoenix cries,
With every beat, a new dawn tries.

The flames leap high, they twist and sway,
A dance of power, come what may.
Such fierce desire fuels the soul,
From blazing heart, we find our role.

Each spark ignites a dormant seed,
With fire's breath, we plant the creed.
In fervent heat, the blossoms swell,
As passion blooms, we weave our spell.

Through trials faced, we claim our might,
With blazing trails, we chase the night.
In molten dreams, we take our stand,
With courage fierce, we clasp fate's hand.

The ember's warmth, our guiding star,
Through darkest times, we'll wander far.
In unity, our voices rise,
From hearts of fire, we touch the skies.

Spirals of Resilience in the Flame

In spiraled ways, the forest breathes,
Where ancient trees, in wisdom, weave.
Through trials deep, their roots entwine,
A tapestry where dreams align.

In every branch, a story grows,
Of whispered winds, and gentle throes.
With fire's kiss, they find their way,
In swirling dance, they shape the day.

Each flicker's path, a lesson true,
From ashes soared, a world anew.
In flames of change, they bravely sway,
A symphony of life at play.

Through swirling trials, they've been forged,
In flickering light, their hearts are gorged.
The spiral winds, our lives entwined,
In fiery loops, our paths aligned.

Resilience glows in every hue,
As flames embrace the morning dew.
With twisted grace, we rise with pride,
In spirals formed, our hopes abide.

Branches of Renewal in the Inferno

From blazing core, new branches reach,
In bursts of life, the heart will teach.
In fiery storms, they twist and bend,
Each noble arc, a tale to send.

With strength they grow, through scorched terrain,
In wildfire's dance, they hide the pain.
From charred remains, they pull up high,
With branches strong, they touch the sky.

In raging heat, they stretch and yawn,
A dance of life, the new day dawns.
With fierce resolve, they stand so tall,
Embracing change, they heed the call.

In storms of fire, they find their grace,
Through trials faced, they hold their place.
Each branch, a tale of love and loss,
From inferno's grip, they count the cost.

Renewed they stand, with hearts ablaze,
In shadows cast, they softly graze.
With every leaf, a promise borne,
From fire's clutch, a new life's sworn.

Flickers of Growth Within

In shadows deep where secrets throng,
The heart's soft whisper spins a song.
A flicker glows beneath the stone,
Emerging strength, once overgrown.

The roots entwined in dark embrace,
Seek light beyond the hidden space.
With every tear, a seed is sown,
Resilience blooms where pain has flown.

Through trials faced, the spirit bends,
Yet in the ache, the courage mends.
For from the depths, true beauty sprouts,
In flickers bright, we find our routes.

Like phoenix flight through smoky haze,
Emerging strong in brilliant blaze.
Each struggle stirs the soul awake,
In flickers bright, our hearts remake.

So cherish all the cracks we bear,
In every loss, there's love to share.
For growth resides within the pain,
In flickers of hope, we rise again.

Patterns in the Ashen Canvas

Upon the ground where ashes lie,
Fractals dance beneath the sky.
Patterns weave in shades of gray,
Stories told in disarray.

The remnants of a fire's spree,
Reveal a truth, a tapestry.
In silence, secrets come alive,
From ashen dreams, the past will thrive.

Each line, a map of years gone past,
In transient forms, our shadows cast.
The beauty in the burnt remains,
Whispers of what still sustains.

Though flames may fade and embers cool,
The heart ignites where hope's the fuel.
For in the depths of loss, we find,
The patterns of the heart and mind.

So lift your gaze from charred despair,
Embrace the art that lingers there.
In every pattern, life unfolds,
A canvas rich with stories told.

Whorls of Existence Rekindled

In spirals bright where shadows twine,
The whorls of life, a grand design.
Each curve a dance, a tale to weave,
In every twist, we still believe.

The winds of change, they pulse and breathe,
As time unveils what hearts conceive.
In circles drawn with tender grace,
We find the spark, our rightful place.

From follies past, new pathways surge,
In whorls of fate, our hopes emerge.
The labyrinthine paths we roam,
Through winding turns, we find our home.

Embrace the flow, the ebb, the tide,
In every whorl, let dreams reside.
For life, a spiral, ever turning,
With every step, a new flame burning.

So gather strength from every turn,
In whorls of existence, brightly burn.
For in the journey, truth will shine,
And rekindle hearts, forever align.

Revelations in the Fragments of Fire

In flickers bright and shadows tall,
Revelations whisper through the hall.
Fragments dance in molten glow,
From ashes high, true insights flow.

The fire's tale, a tapestry spun,
Of battles fought and victories won.
In every spark, a truth ignites,
To guide our souls on starry nights.

What once was whole can still be found,
In scattered pieces, life's unbound.
From shards of pain, new visions bloom,
In fire's embrace, we shed our gloom.

So let the flames reveal your worth,
In whispered vows, rediscover birth.
For in the fragments, wisdom thrives,
In every ember, hope strives.

Embrace the fire, let spirits grow,
Beyond the loss, let passion flow.
In revelations, hearts inspire,
From fragments once, we rise entire.

Spirals of Change in Fiery Ash

In the heart of the blaze, new life awakes,
From the warmth of the ashes, a promise makes.
Whispers of hope in the crackling fire,
Spirals of change dance, igniting desire.

Shadows of dusk paint the swirling ash,
Each ember a story, a fleeting flash.
Beneath the surface, the soul transforms,
Resilient spirits break free from their norms.

As the winds carry murmurs, they soar and glide,
In the depths of the darkness, they find their guide.
With each leap of faith, they shatter the night,
Embracing the chaos, they set forth in light.

Fires may consume, but rebirth is near,
From the cinders arise the dreams we hold dear.
In spirals of change, our destinies weave,
Through the trials of ash, we learn to believe.

The Anatomy of a Second Chance

Fiddles of fate play a somber tune,
Yet hope still dances beneath the moon.
With every misstep, a lesson learned,
In the quiet moments, our spirits turned.

Like phoenixes rising from paths once crossed,
In the anatomy of loss, gains are embossed.
Pulses beat stronger with time's gentle hand,
Finding solace in places that's hard to understand.

Threads of regret softly woven in gold,
A tapestry rich, each story retold.
In the shadows of doubt, new lights emerge,
A chance to create, to fix and to purge.

With courage as armor, and dreams as our guide,
We traverse the valleys, hearts open wide.
Every breath, every heartbeat, a brand-new chance,
In the rhythm of life, we learn to dance.

Unknown Growths from Charred Soil

In the remnants of ruin, secrets lie bare,
From the charred earth's embrace, life dares to care.
Roots stretch below, unseen and alive,
In the heart of despair, new hopes will thrive.

With patience, we nurture the fractured remains,
As dreams take their shape amidst all the strains.
From the depths of anguish, sprouts push through,
Each tender green promise a glimpse of the new.

In silence, they grow, breaking free of their chains,
The echoes of labor in soft moonlit gains.
Through struggle and strife, they stretch toward the sky,
As the past fades away, only futures reply.

Amongst ashen ruins, resilience will bloom,
Casting away shadows, dispelling all gloom.
With every small victory, hope intertwines,
In the unknown growths, our trust realigns.

Echoes of Creation in Flame

In the crackle of fire, the whispers arise,
Echoes of creation, with luminous eyes.
Shadows pirouette, as the flames start to sing,
In the heart of the blaze, we embrace everything.

With every flicker, a history's told,
Of dreams igniting, of futures bold.
From ashes to embers, a dance intertwines,
In the song of the flame, the universe shines.

As the night sways gently, revealing its grace,
We gather the sparks, our fears we displace.
Through warmth and light, our spirits ascend,
In echoes of fire, we find our true friends.

And when the last breath of the evening arrives,
In the embers we see how passion survives.
Together we stand, as shadows grow long,
In the melodies woven, we find where we belong.

Gnarled Roots of Defiance

In the shadowed woods they dwell,
With roots that twist, and tales to tell.
A strength unfurls beneath the ground,
Where whispered truths in silence sound.

Against the storms, they stand so bold,
Defying whispers that grow cold.
With every branch that seeks the sky,
They grasp for dreams that never die.

Each gnarled twist born of the night,
A dance of shadows, fierce and bright.
In tangled paths, their hearts ablaze,
They carve out life in daring ways.

When darkness speaks in ancient tongue,
These roots reply, forever young.
Through withering years they shall endure,
A testament to hearts so pure.

With every storm, they grow anew,
Defying fate, forging their view.
In nature's song, their voices rise,
A chorus strong beneath the skies.

Rebirth in the Embers

From ashes black, a spark takes flight,
A flicker born within the night.
It dances soft on fragile breeze,
Whispers fate with gentle ease.

The warmth of dreams in shadows bright,
A phoenix sings of endless light.
Through charred remains, new life will bloom,
Casting aside all past's dark gloom.

With every ember, hope ignites,
A tapestry of fiery lights.
Resilient hearts, they gather near,
Awakening the buried fear.

In swirling smoke, they find their way,
To rise anew, embrace the day.
With trembling wings, they soar and fly,
A symphony against the sky.

From embers' glow, the tale unfolds,
Of warmth and love in courage bold.
Through trials faced, they find the grace,
To weave the magic of this place.

Seeds of Hope Amongst the Ash

In silence deep where shadows linger,
Seeds of hope fall, soft as a whisper.
Amongst the ash, they seek the sun,
Determined hearts, forever spun.

Each tiny dot, a promise pure,
In cracked earth waits a future sure.
With every drop of morning dew,
They break the ground; they start anew.

In whispered dreams, they find their voice,
Offering a chance, a brand new choice.
Through every crack, they push and strive,
In the dance of life, they will survive.

When shadows loom and darkness spreads,
They rise up high, banishing dread.
A tapestry of green reborn,
From ashen wisps, new life is worn.

So let the past be but a guide,
For seeds of hope will never hide.
In every heart, they take their stand,
A future bright, a promised land.

The Language of Heat and Renewal

Beneath the surface, whispers hum,
A language where the wild things come.
In every crack, the spirit speaks,
With fiery warmth, the heart it seeks.

The language flows like molten gold,
In tales of warmth that are retold.
Through heat and flame, life's song is sung,
And in this dance, the world is young.

Each flicker tells of past and birth,
Of deep connections rooted in earth.
In ashes left by time's cruel hand,
Emergence calls back to the land.

So let the fire crack and roar,
For from its heart, we will restore.
The language of the brave and true,
In every heart, it starts anew.

From flickering glow to radiant blaze,
We find our path through life's great maze.
In heat's embrace, we learn to stand,
And weave our tales across the land.

Waves of Transformation in Fire

In the midst of shadows cast,
Waves of change begin to rise,
Fire dances, free and vast,
Igniting dreams beneath the skies.

Crimson embers whisper loud,
In the heart of ancient lore,
Every spark, a glowing shroud,
Waves that beckon evermore.

From the ashes of despair,
New beginnings softly bloom,
In the warmth, the world lays bare,
Transformation finds its room.

Catch the fire in your soul,
Let it guide your endless flight,
Waves of fate, they spin and roll,
Leading you to radiant light.

Embrace the warmth, the fierce embrace,
In the chaos, truth will show,
Waves of fire, a sacred space,
Where paths converge and spirits grow.

Unraveling Life from the Ashen Core

In the depths of hardened stone,
Lies a promise wrapped in grey,
Unraveling, a life unknown,
From the core where shadows play.

Burned and broken, yet alive,
Hope emerges through the cracks,
In the silence, dreams will strive,
Finding light where nothing lacks.

Softly whispered tales await,
In the stillness, secrets soar,
Ashen dust cannot abate,
Life will reach from every pore.

Feel the pulse beneath the skin,
As the fire reshapes the mold,
Unraveling begins within,
A journey brave, a story bold.

From the rubble, rise anew,
Every challenge, every scar,
In the ashes, life breaks through,
Guided by a shining star.

The Essence of Life in the Glow

In twilight's soft and soothing shade,
The essence of life begins to bloom,
Each heartbeat's rhythm, a serenade,
Illuminating shadows of the room.

A flicker like a distant star,
In the glow, our spirits dance,
Whispers echo from afar,
Calling forth our hearts to prance.

Moments treasured, held so dear,
In this light, we find our voice,
Embracing joy, confronting fear,
In the glow, we make our choice.

Every breath a flickering flame,
In the essence, we unite,
Though the world may not feel the same,
Together, we burn ever bright.

The glow transcends the darkest night,
A bond that cannot be undone,
In the essence, we find our might,
Together, we are always one.

Twisted Origins of the Burning Heart

Within the depths of tangled roots,
A burning heart begins to weave,
Twisted paths and bitter fruits,
Secrets hidden, none perceive.

From the ashes, stories rise,
Of a fire forged in pain,
With every tear, the spirit cries,
Yet in darkness, hope won't wane.

Winds of fate, they twist and twine,
Carving destinies unseen,
In the heart, a pulse divine,
A journey fierce, a life serene.

Echoes of the past remain,
In the chambers of the soul,
Twisted origins, we feel the strain,
Yet the fire makes us whole.

Through the flames, we seek the light,
Embracing all that life imparts,
In the shadows, fierce and bright,
We discover our burning hearts.

Tendrils of Life in the Fiery Void

In shadows deep, where darkness sings,
The tendrils stir, embracing wings.
A flicker bright, a spark divine,
Life's whispered dance in the heart of time.

From ashes cold, the promise grows,
Through fiery realms where no one knows.
With every breath, hope intertwines,
Crafting a tale where fate aligns.

Against the blaze, resilience stands,
Each glowing ember in daring hands.
A tapestry forged in trials bold,
In fiery voids, our stories told.

In darkest night, when all seems lost,
The tendrils weave, no matter the cost.
With courage drawn from depths of pain,
Life blooms anew, as love remains.

So here we stand, 'neath stars aligned,
In fiery voids where light is blind.
Together we forge, together we rise,
In tendrils of life, we touch the skies.

Flourish Amidst the Char

In charred remains where hopes have burned,
New visions rise, their fates discerned.
With tender roots in ash and stone,
We flourish bright, no longer alone.

Each flick of flame ignites the dream,
A vibrant pulse, a fervent beam.
Through shattered silence, we will sing,
For every loss, a new hope springs.

Amidst the char, the soul takes flight,
To dance with shadows, seek the light.
The past may haunt, yet we embrace,
In every scar, a tale of grace.

With every beat, our spirits grow,
From charred remains, a radiant glow.
Resilience wrapped in nature's art,
We bloom as one, each vibrant heart.

So let us thrive where ashes lay,
To paint the world in shades of play.
In every crack, resilience shows,
We flourish bright, as courage flows.

The Unseen Life Beneath the Heat

Beneath the surface, whispers call,
In muted tones, they rise and fall.
The unseen life, a hidden thread,
In warmth of hearth, where dreams are fed.

Through smoky veils, the secrets hide,
In embered glow, they twist and glide.
Each pulsing heart, ignites the night,
A spark of hope, a blaze of light.

With every crackle, sorrows flee,
As unseen life begins to be.
In shadows deep, our courage swells,
To weave the tales that time compels.

From silent depths, a symphony sounds,
In fiery realms where life abounds.
Unseen, yet felt, the magic grows,
In every moment, the spirit glows.

So heed the whispers 'neath the heat,
The unseen life is bittersweet.
In every struggle, there's a chance,
To feel the pulse of fate's advance.

Budding Dreams from Cinders

From cinders gray, a whisper stirs,
Soft tender dreams, like gentle purrs.
In cryptic gleam, they seek the dawn,
With every breath, a new life drawn.

Amidst the ruins, visions bloom,
From ashes rise, dispelling gloom.
Budding hopes with colors bright,
Illuminate the endless night.

Through fragile steps, we navigate,
The budding dreams, our destined fate.
And in their glow, we find our way,
Through cinders cold to warmth of day.

Each ember cradles tender wishes,
A dance of fate, where heart still swishes.
Beneath the weight, we find our song,
From cinders rise, where we belong.

So let the dreams like blossoms soar,
From cinders fierce, we seek for more.
In every heart, a spark will gleam,
For life begins with budding dream.

Curved Shadows in the Ember

In the twilight where whispers wane,
Curved shadows dance, free from pain.
They twist and turn, a silent art,
Etching secrets, heart to heart.

The ember glows with fiery grace,
A fleeting moment, a hidden trace.
Echoes of laughter, soft and low,
In the warmth of the fire, the old tales grow.

Silent companions, these ghostly forms,
Weaving through nights, outsmarting storms.
In the flicker, a world unfolds,
Of dreams once lost and stories told.

A tapestry spun from light and dark,
In every ember, a spark, a mark.
Bound by the ties that flicker and sway,
While shadows curve, and night warms the day.

So linger here, in the gentle glow,
Where time stands still, and love will flow.
With every breath drawn near the flame,
Curved shadows whisper your name.

The Heart of a Reborn Flame

From ashes cold, a heartbeat wakes,
In the depth of night, the magic takes.
With a spark, the courage starts,
Revealing the dreams held in hidden parts.

Flickering bright, the flame does rise,
Exhaling warmth like starlit skies.
It dances slowly, a mystical show,
Lighting the path for hearts that glow.

In the flicker, a story beckons,
Of lost, of found, of ancient sections.
Embers rain like twinkling stars,
Painting the night with the warmth of scars.

For every breath, a promise new,
In the heart of the flame, a world in view.
With hope reborn in the night's embrace,
The whisper of softly woven grace.

So cherish the light, hold it dear,
For in every flame, there's beauty sheer.
In the heart of the fire, life will reclaim,
The love that dwells in the reborn flame.

Nature's Puzzle in the Smoke

In the rising smoke, a puzzle laid,
Nature's whispers, never afraid.
With each tendril, a story speaks,
In the silent language of forest peaks.

The intricate dance of shapes alive,
Where countless mysteries thrive.
An echo of life, both near and far,
It brings together, like threads from a star.

A tapestry spun from earth and air,
In every swirl, a secret to share.
Through the veil, the world transforms,
Embracing change as the chaos warms.

The smoke weaves tales of days gone by,
Of laughter, of sorrow, of every sigh.
In nature's hands, so wise and grand,
The puzzle grows, a mystical strand.

So pause and ponder, let it unfold,
The stories untold, the truths of old.
In the smoke, find the whispers of fate,
Nature's puzzle waits to translate.

Beneath the Surface of the Blaze

Beneath the fire, a world concealed,
Where dreams and whispers are revealed.
The crackling beats a rhythmic song,
Pulling us closer, where we belong.

It's a dance of shadows, a flickering light,
Creating wonders in the depth of night.
Hidden tales glide softly, unseen,
In the blaze's heart, where spirits convene.

With every flicker, a moment burns bright,
In this silent chamber of shimmering light.
Frosted echoes of a past divine,
In the heart of the blaze, fate intertwines.

So gather round and listen well,
To the secrets hidden within the swell.
For beneath the surface, the fire reveals,
A tapestry woven with love that heals.

Let the flames show you the way inside,
Where the heart of the blaze can't hide.
In the warmth of the glow, feel time embrace,
Beneath the surface, we find our place.

Nature's Touch in Charred Silence

In shadows dark, the trees now sigh,
Their whispers lost, beneath the sky.
Yet in the ashes, life will creep,
Awakening dreams that nature keeps.

A million sparks in twilight gleam,
As grass breaks through the ashen seam.
With gentle light, the dawn will show,
The hope that lingers, soft and slow.

The streams will hum a hushed refrain,
As petals greet the warm spring rain.
In charred remains, a promise stays,
To brush the darkness with its rays.

Behold the roots in silence grow,
A tapestry of life in tow.
Amidst the blackened, burned-out past,
New colors bloom, their beauty vast.

And as the sun begins its climb,
We learn from loss, embrace the time.
For nature's touch can mend and heal,
In every scar, new life reveals.

The Tender Roots of a Fiery Blossom

In embered earth, a secret stirs,
A tender root, where hope occurs.
From fiery depths, the shoot will rise,
To greet the warmth of painted skies.

Where flames once danced, a lullaby,
To nature's song, the heart will sigh.
Each petal soft, like whispers shared,
In every breeze, a dream declared.

The fiery bloom, a daring might,
Against the darkness, it finds light.
A symbol bold of life's embrace,
In charred remains, it finds its place.

With colors bright, the world adorned,
Old scars now weave a tale reborn.
Through every trial, resilience grows,
In the tender roots, true strength shows.

So let the winds of change come through,
For fiery blooms can start anew.
With each new dawn, a promise made,
In nature's grace, all fears will fade.

Echoes of Life in Scorched Soil

In scorched soil, whispers call,
A hidden world stands proud and tall.
From blackened ground, the echoes play,
Of life that thrived, then slipped away.

Among the char, in silence deep,
The roots remember, secrets keep.
Each flicker of the fading light,
A tale of struggle, of endless fight.

Life cradles dreams beneath the pain,
For every loss, there's hope to gain.
In ashes gray, the heart will find,
Resilience born of nature's kind.

Through every wound, a lesson learned,
In every spark, a heart that burned.
So let the soil drink the rain,
In echoes lost, let love remain.

For from the depths of all that's lost,
New life will rise, despite the cost.
In every dance of sun and moon,
The echoes of life will softly croon.

Awakening from the Depths of Embers

From depths of embers, warmth will rise,
A dance of shadows, where magic lies.
In silence held, the whispers call,
Of ancient tales that bind us all.

With every ember, hope ignites,
Beneath the stars on velvet nights.
Awakening dreams from ashes gray,
To greet the dawn in golden spray.

Each breath a promise, woven tight,
In murmured thoughts, we seek the light.
For every trial faced in dusk,
Can lead us to the dawn of trust.

The soil holds stories yet untold,
In flames that flicker, hearts unfold.
From depth to height, in life's embrace,
We find our strength, our rightful place.

So let the embers guide the way,
To brighter paths, to new array.
Awakening hearts, with every spark,
In unity, we light the dark.

Breathing in the Glow of Change

In the whisper of the dawn, where shadows fade,
Hope dances lightly, a shimmering cascade.
With every breath, a promise begins to loom,
Transformation blossoms, dispelling the gloom.

Petals unfurl, embracing the warm new light,
Casting aside sorrow, eager to take flight.
The heart beats softly, a drum of the bold,
In the glow of change, stories unfold.

Threads of the past weave into the now,
Each moment a lesson, a sacred vow.
Shimmering visions drift through the mind,
In the embrace of the future, we find.

With wings made of stardust, we rise and soar,
The journey of daring, we endlessly explore.
In the breath of today, tomorrow ignites,
Breathing in change, we welcome the heights.

Together we stand, on this threshold of fate,
With courage as our shield, we navigate.
Embracing the unknown, with spirits aglow,
In the magic of life, we choose how to grow.

Currents of Life Within the Ash

In the stillness of night, where embers reside,
Life hums in whispers, though dreams may hide.
Beneath the grey surface, a flicker remains,
The pulse of creation, joy wrapped in chains.

From ashes departed, fresh beginnings arise,
Tales of renewal weave through the skies.
A spark ignites passion, as shadows take flight,
Currents of life dance, chasing the light.

An ancient refrain echoes soft in the dark,
With each rising heartbeat, we kindle the spark.
A tapestry rich, threaded with hope's thread,
From dust we are made, by dreams we are led.

Through valleys of sorrow, our spirits must climb,
In the depths of despair, there's beauty in time.
The cycle of life, a continuous flow,
In the heart of the ash, the essence will grow.

So let us remember, in silence, we birth,
From the ashes of pain, there's newfound worth.
Embrace every moment with love and with grace,
In the currents of life, we discover our place.

The Rhythm of Resurgence

In the quietest hour before the day wakes,
A heartbeat awakens, the stillness it shakes.
Whispers of longing entwine with the breeze,
The rhythm of resurgence flows with such ease.

Each dawn is a promise, a sweet serenade,
The past gently lingers but cannot invade.
Promises gathered, like petals in spring,
We rise with the sun, our souls take to wing.

In shadows we wandered, in echoes we dreamed,
Yet hope is a river, unbound and unseamed.
With courage our compass, we chart out our course,
In the dance of the tides, we discover our force.

The pulse of the earth beats beneath our bare feet,
Uniting our essence, our past and defeat.
With every heartbeat, a story unfolds,
The rhythm of resurgence, the magic it holds.

So let us rejoice, in the cycle we dwell,
In the heart of the tempest, we flourish and swell.
Together we rise, in harmony's song,
The rhythm of resurgence carries us along.

Courting the Fire's Caress

In the glow of the embers, where shadows entwine,
We dance with the flames, our spirits align.
Courting the fire's caress, wild and free,
A flicker of passion ignites in the sea.

With laughter like starlight, we twirl in the night,
Embracing the chaos, surrendering fright.
Each spark a reminder of moments we crave,
The warmth of connection, a bond that we save.

As the night stretches on, with secrets laid bare,
We weave stories deeper, with love in the air.
In the glow of the fire, darkness bows low,
Courting the flames, we let our hearts show.

With each flickering jest, each tale we exchange,
New worlds come alive, through courage we change.
In the heart of the fire, we summon our truth,
Reclaiming our dreams, the wonder of youth.

So let us embrace, in the blaze of the now,
In the warmth of the fire, take one solemn vow.
Together we stand, through the night and the day,
Courting the fire's caress, we'll find our way.

Fiery Echoes of a Green Heart

In the depths where shadows weave,
A pulse of life dares to believe.
Embers dance in silent play,
Whispers of hope, come what may.

Roots entwined in sacred earth,
Spirits rise, proclaiming birth.
Fires rage, yet green prevails,
Nature's strength, weaves vibrant trails.

With each flicker, dreams take flight,
Guided by the stars at night.
Through the ash, a truth unspoken,
Echoes of love, never broken.

Beneath the blaze, a secret song,
Of starlit journeys, deep and long.
Fingers reach for skies unknown,
In every heart, a seed is sown.

So let the fires burn and rage,
For from the flames, we turn the page.
With every loss, a flame anew,
Fiery echoes will guide us through.

The Flourish Beneath the Inferno

Amid the chaos, life takes hold,
In flames of red, a tale unfolds.
Leaves flicker 'neath the heated glare,
Yet from the fury, moments rare.

Roots push forth through molten stone,
In a dance, they find their own.
Stars above in twilight's gaze,
Guide the green in endless phase.

Daring blooms in ashes rise,
Kissed by fire, they touch the skies.
The heart of nature, fierce and bold,
A story of life, brightly told.

Voices call from smokey trails,
A melody where courage sails.
Each petal whispers life's sweet truth,
Beneath the inferno, lies our youth.

So let the flames engulf the night,
For in their warmth, we find our light.
The flourish blooms, while embers fade,
In the heart of earth, hope is made.

Life's Reclamation from the Flames

From charred bones of yesterday,
New dreams awaken, find their way.
Hope unfolds with every dawn,
Nature's heart, forever drawn.

Fires rage but cannot quell,
The stories that the ancients tell.
In the ashes, soft whispers grow,
Seeds of promise begin to show.

With strength anew, we rise again,
From tangled roots, we break the chain.
Each flicker calls to those who lost,
Life's reclamation, worth the cost.

Through fiery trials and bitter nights,
The spirit thrives, ignites the sights.
In every tear, a river flows,
From the flames, a garden grows.

So dare to dream, to forge anew,
From burning depths, life's dreams ensue.
With open hearts, we shall reclaim,
The essence of our fiery flame.

Whispers of Growth Amidst the Ash

In the quiet of the smoldering night,
Whispers echo, soft and light.
Amidst the ash, the green finds way,
Guiding lost souls, come what may.

Fingers stretch through ashen dust,
Trust in nature's gentle thrust.
Each breath taken, a promise spoken,
In fragile truths, hearts are unbroken.

The dance of life, so sweet, so frail,
Unfolds its wings, begins to sail.
Soft colors bloom, where darkness lies,
Promises linger, beneath gray skies.

From every ember, a story weaves,
Of growing hopes, and gently leaves.
Touch the soil, for life shall rise,
In whispered strength, a new surprise.

So fear not flames, nor bitter ash,
For in the heart, dreams fiercely dash.
Whispers of growth, a gentle call,
Amidst the ash, we rise from fall.

Scars of Growth Reimagined

In shadows deep where secrets dwell,
A tale of scars begins to swell.
Through trials faced, the heart does bloom,
From wounds anew, dispelling gloom.

Each mark a story, wisdom sown,
A silent strength in flesh and bone.
With every tear, a chance to rise,
To see the world through wiser eyes.

In whispered winds, the past will speak,
Of battles fought and futures bleak.
Yet through the pain, a light unfolds,
A tapestry of dreams retold.

The journey's path, though fraught with strife,
Shapes the essence of this life.
Embrace the scars, let healing start,
For growth transforms the tender heart.

So let each line upon your skin,
Be proof of strength that lies within.
As blossoms bloom from darkest night,
A garden thrives in morning light.

The Dance of Life from Ash

In realms where fire met despair,
The phoenix rises from the air.
With wings of gold, in splendor bright,
It dances forth into the light.

From ashes cold, a story told,
Of trials faced and courage bold.
The rhythm flows, the heartbeats pound,
As life emerges from the ground.

Each flicker glows, a spark of hope,
Through darkest nights, we learn to cope.
With every step, the flames ignite,
Illuminating shadows' plight.

Together bound by fate's design,
A symphony of souls align.
In grace, we twirl, in fate we trust,
From loss to life, we rise from dust.

So let the dance of flames endure,
A testament, fierce and pure.
For from the ash, new dreams will spring,
In every heart, the fire's sing.

Resilient Threads in the Fire

The loom of life weaves tight and true,
With threads of gold, and shades of blue.
In every strand, a tale unfolds,
Of strength and grace in hearts so bold.

Through trials faced within the flame,
Resilience rises, not the same.
Transforming pain to vibrant thread,
A fabric rich where dreams are spread.

In every knot, a lesson learned,
From fragile hopes, brave spirits burned.
Yet in the heat, creation thrives,
As woven hearts embrace their lives.

The tapestry, a work of art,
Stitched by the hands that know the heart.
In fiery depths, we find our place,
A testament to love and grace.

So let the threads entwine and blend,
In every heart, where hopes commend.
For from the fire, we shall arise,
Resilient souls, to touch the skies.

The Void Beneath the Flame

Beneath the blaze, a silent void,
Where echoes dwell, and dreams are buoyed.
In shadows cast by flickering light,
A hidden realm embraces night.

The embers burn, yet still we seek,
The truth within the hushed mystique.
In depths unknown, we find our way,
Through whispered fears, to break the fray.

For every flicker, every spark,
Illuminates the quiet dark.
In voids we learn to stand our ground,
And find the strength that's always found.

The flame may dance with wild embrace,
Yet in the stillness, we find grace.
A paradox where shadows play,
This void, a guide that shows the way.

So in the dark, let courage grow,
To face the flame, to feel the glow.
For in the vastness, we ignite,
A flame reborn, a boundless light.

Resilience in the Wake of Ashes

In shadows deep, where darkness clings,
A will persists, as the heart still sings.
For every end, a spark ignites,
In courage found, hope takes flight.

The ashes whisper tales of old,
Of battles fought, of scars turned gold.
Each tear shed, a seed is sown,
In grief and joy, our strength is grown.

Among the ruins, green may sprout,
With roots that grip and twist about.
The time to rise is never far,
From fallen dreams, we reach the stars.

With every challenge, we'll take a stance,
In trials faced, we find our chance.
In the wake of all that's lost,
Resilience blooms, no matter the cost.

So gather strength, as seasons shift,
In every darkness, find the gift.
And from the ashes, life shall beam,
In unity formed, we weave a dream.

The Resurgence of Hidden Vines

Beneath the soil, where secrets lie,
The hidden vines reach for the sky.
With silence loud, they push and cling,
Awakening life to gently spring.

Through cracks of stone, they make their way,
In quiet strength, they know no sway.
Against the odds they twist and turn,
With each small leaf, the passion burns.

From shadowed depths to golden light,
The hidden vines emerge in might.
In grace, they sway, in beauty weave,
Their tenacity is hard to believe.

An emerald cloak on barren ground,
A stubborn heart where hope is found.
They teach us all to be aware,
Of life's resilience, strong and rare.

So let the hidden vines inspire,
For growth comes forth in heart's desire.
In muted thorns, there lies a song,
Of flourishing where we belong.

From Embered Remains, New Beginnings

From embered remains where darkness spreads,
New beginnings bloom, like threads unspun.
In frozen night, a promise threads,
Renewal whispers, the day has won.

With every loss, a lesson learned,
In ash and soot, our hopes discerned.
The fire dims, but cannot die,
In fragile hearts, the flames still fly.

A phoenix rises with wings of grace,
From smoky dreams, we find our place.
Through trials deep, we claim our worth,
In every end, we toast to birth.

With colors bright, we paint the air,
In every heartbeat, love laid bare.
For after dark, the dawn shall break,
A symphony of sound we make.

Embrace the scars, the tales they spin,
For every end births where we begin.
From embered remains, let hope ignite,
In every soul, a precious light.

Tender Growth in a Scorched Realm

In landscapes burned by fire's embrace,
Tender growth begins to trace.
With fragile shoots, the green does strive,
To find a way, to feel alive.

Amidst the wreckage, life persists,
With gentle strength, it coexists.
The sun spills warmth on charred remains,
And from the grief, new hope gains.

Tiny buds in blackened clay,
Against the odds, they find their say.
With every drop of rain that falls,
The tender growth recalls its calls.

So bless the ground, once burned and bare,
For life can rise from deep despair.
In every seed, a tale is spun,
Of tender growth in endless sun.

And as the seasons come and go,
We bloom anew, our spirits flow.
For in the scorched, there's beauty found,
In life's embrace, we are unbound.

The Unseen Marvel of Renewal

In the stillness of night's embrace,
Nature breathes a hidden grace.
From ashes rise the dreams anew,
A canvas painted in every hue.

Beneath the frost, the seeds lie still,
Awaiting time's enchanting thrill.
With whispers soft, the earth awakes,
A wondrous dance, as silence breaks.

Gentle rains and the sun's soft kiss,
Awaken all that one might miss.
From barren ground, hope starts to sprout,
A testament to endurance, no doubt.

As days grow long, and shadows fade,
The steadfast spirit shall not be swayed.
In each small bud, a story sings,
Of life that blossoms, as joy it brings.

So let us honor this miracle rare,
The unseen marvel that fills the air.
For in each ending, a beginning waits,
A tapestry woven by fate's own gates.

Spirals of New Beginnings

Like whispers woven through the trees,
New beginnings dance upon the breeze.
In spirals bright, the world unwinds,
Each moment cherished, love defines.

From gentle seeds, new journeys start,
An endless cycle, a work of art.
With every leaf, a tale unfolds,
Of courage found and dreams retold.

The sun climbs high, the shadows shift,
In every turn, the spirits lift.
Through swirling paths, we find our way,
In the heart of night, the dawn will play.

So rise and twirl in joy profound,
Embrace the magic that's all around.
For life's a spiral, bright and free,
A wondrous journey, meant to be.

With open hearts, we take the chance,
In every step, a sacred dance.
Spirals of new beginnings thrive,
In every soul, the spark alive.

Echoes of Heat and Life

In the silence, warmth does glow,
Echoes of heat that softly flow.
Embers flicker in muted night,
A cradle for the stars so bright.

In each heartbeat, the fire sings,
Of ancient tales and wondrous things.
The sparks leap high, reaching dreams,
In shadows cast, the magic gleams.

Life pulses in the glowing shade,
Where moments cherished are never made.
Through fiery trails and starlit skies,
Love ignites, where hope never dies.

Let echoes dance, a rhythm true,
In every bond, the spark renews.
For life's a tapestry of light,
Woven by passion, warm and bright.

In every breath, the flames reside,
In warmth we trust, never to hide.
Echoes of heat, in hearts remain,
A timeless cycle, love's sweet gain.

Fragile Strength in the Warmth

In the glow of a soft embrace,
Fragile strength finds its rightful place.
Amidst the chaos, calm resides,
Within the heart where true love hides.

Like petals soft on morning dew,
There's power in the gentle view.
With every sigh, a whisper grows,
In tranquil moments, resilience shows.

The roots run deep, though branches sway,
In warmth we find the light of day.
Through trials faced and storms that pass,
The spirit shines, like polished glass.

Embrace the tender, hold it tight,
For fragile strength ignites the night.
In love's embrace, we find our way,
A beacon shining, come what may.

So let us nurture what we hold,
In warmth's embrace, be brave and bold.
For in the fragile lies the might,
A dance of shadows, love's true light.

Surreal Growth in a Fiery Landscape

Amidst the flames where shadows dance,
New life emerges, a curious chance.
Leaves of sapphire twist and twine,
In the heart of chaos, magic aligns.

Blazing sun with a gentle kiss,
Paints the world, a fiery bliss.
Roots dig deeper in ash and soot,
From the wreckage, green shoots shoot.

Whispers of willows through the smoke,
Nature's resilience, a promise woke.
Each petal carries a tale untold,
In this furnace, bravery enfolded.

Among the ruins, life does thrive,
In each ember, dreams contrive.
Colors burst like a vivid scheme,
In a surreal, fiery dream.

Transformation blooms in bright array,
Defying night in the light of day.
With every spark, a story grows,
In this landscape, where wonder flows.

The Pulse of Renewal Deep Beneath

In the earth's embrace, a heartbeat hums,
Whispers of life where silence comes.
Beneath the surface, secrets churn,
In the darkened depths, the lanterns burn.

Roots of old tales twist and weave,
In the soil, all that we believe.
Silent flickers of hope arise,
As change unfolds beneath the skies.

A cradle of dreams, buried yet bright,
In the stillness, preparing for flight.
Emerging softly, like dawn's first light,
The pulse of renewal in endless night.

Each heartbeat echoes a timeless song,
In the depths where the brave belong.
Hope dances lightly, chases despair,
Through the breathing earth, everywhere.

From the depths, the world will bloom,
Cradling life in the darkened gloom.
The pulse of nature forever persists,
In the cycle of life, no moment missed.

Melodies of Phoenix' Touch

From ashes rises a song anew,
A dance of flames, a radiant view.
With every note, the embers swell,
A phoenix' chorus begins to tell.

Golden wings in the evening air,
Singing stories of loss and dare.
Through trials forged in a fiery breath,
Life serenades the dance of death.

Cadences echo in twilight hues,
Whispers carried on vibrant blues.
With each rise, a promise bestowed,
In the heart of fire, the light has glowed.

Melodies twine in the dusky light,
Cradling dreams in the quiet night.
With each refrain, the past surrenders,
To a future bright, where hope remembers.

Sparks of brilliance fill the sky,
With every note, the spirits fly.
In the concert of life, we find our way,
In melodies sung at the break of day.

Hidden Journeys in Scorched Earth

In the barren land where courage stands,
Hidden journeys weave through shifting sands.
With every step, the ground does sigh,
As whispers travel to the sky.

Footprints linger in the dust,
Each path a testament of trust.
Amongst the thorns, the roses bloom,
In this scorched earth, life finds room.

Secrets buried in the heat,
Underneath, new adventures greet.
With every burn, a story breaks,
In the landscape where the heart awakes.

Beneath the pain, a spark ignites,
Sowing hope in the darkest nights.
The journey flows, a river deep,
In fragile soil, the dreams we keep.

Through trials fierce, the spirit soars,
In hidden journeys, life restores.
From scorched earth, we rise anew,
An endless journey, brave and true.

Whispers of Resilience

In shadows deep, where hopes reside,
A flicker glows, with strength inside.
Through storms of doubt, we make our way,
With whispers soft, we greet the day.

The night may wail, the winds may howl,
But from each bruise, we wear a scowl.
Like phoenix rise, we seek the light,
Transforming pain to purest flight.

Beneath the weight of heavy hearts,
The seeds of courage dare to start.
With gentle hands, we till the earth,
And nurture dreams of quiet worth.

So let the echoes guide our feet,
As journey calls, we won't retreat.
In unity, we find our song,
A melody where we belong.

And when the trials bend us low,
We'll stand as one, and bravely grow.
For in the dark, we find our way,
With whispers soft, we'll greet the day.

Fragments of a Fiery Birth

From ashes cold, a spark ignites,
A dance of flames, with wild delights.
In every flicker, stories teem,
Of battles fought and daring dreams.

With each eruption, we take flight,
In vibrant hues, we chase the light.
Our hearts aflame, we shed our fears,
In vivid shades, we dry our tears.

The fire speaks in crackling tones,
Of hope reborn, of ancient bones.
We gather round, in circles tight,
To share the warmth, to feel the night.

And just as night gives way to dawn,
We rise anew, though shadows yawn.
From fiery depths, our voices soar,
In unity, we seek much more.

For all the fragments, fierce and bold,
Are stories shared, and dreams retold.
Through every trial, we proudly stand,
In fiery birth, we make our brand.

Twisted Echoes of Renewal

In tangled woods, perceptions change,
The echoes dance, both strange and strange.
With every turn, a lesson learned,
In twisted paths, our spirits burned.

Through twisted roots and branches wide,
We find the beauty, oft denied.
In shadows thick, we trace our way,
To glimpse the dawn of a brighter day.

The whispers linger, soft and clear,
They guide our hearts and quell our fear.
In broken places, life takes hold,
With tender strength, we'll break the mold.

Each echo tells of hope reborn,
With scars as proof, we face the morn.
In unity, we weave our rhyme,
Through twisted paths, we conquer time.

So let the echoes speak our name,
In every rise, we find our flame.
Through lessons learned and battles won,
In twisted echoes, we become one.

Bumps Beneath the Ashes

Beneath the ashes, life still stirs,
In hidden beats, a pulse concurs.
With every breath, the earth awakes,
As tender buds, the silence breaks.

In rocky beds and rough terrain,
Our hopes emerge from soil and rain.
Through trials steep, we make our stand,
With hands of strength, we form a band.

The bumps we feel, they shape our fate,
In every bruise, a chance to create.
Though life may cast a heavy weight,
Resilience flowers, we celebrate.

With open hearts, we face the storm,
In unity, our spirits warm.
For in the struggles, wisdom grows,
Through bumps beneath, our courage flows.

So let the ashes tell our tale,
Of strength reborn, we shall prevail.
With every step, our spirits fly,
Through bumps beneath, we touch the sky.

Emergent Patterns in the Ruins

In shadows deep where silence weeps,
Petals fall on forgotten keeps.
Amidst the stones, a soft reply,
A tale of hope beneath the sky.

Whispers dance on breezes light,
Painting walls with dreams in flight.
Crumbled bricks tell stories bold,
Of lives once lived, now tales retold.

The ivy clings to ancient art,
A living thread, a beating heart.
Through cracks, new life begins to weave,
In ruins' grace, we dare believe.

Each crack a pathway to the dawn,
From dust and ruin, love is drawn.
What once was lost can still be found,
In vibrant echoes, life resounds.

A symphony of textures bright,
In every hue, the past ignites.
With every falter, rise anew,
In ruins, strength finds birth, it's true.

Visions of Life in the Wreckage

Amid the shards of shattered dreams,
The light breaks through in silver beams.
Where chaos reigned, now quiet lies,
The heart remembers, softly sighs.

In wreckage, seeds of hope are sown,
With every crack, a vision grown.
The once forgotten, now shall thrive,
In whispers low, we feel alive.

A dance of shadows, time unfurls,
In vacant spaces, beauty swirls.
Each wreck a canvas, life's embrace,
Reflecting grace in shattered space.

The air is filled with stories bold,
Of hearts that bled, and dreams retold.
In quiet moments, we shall see,
The strength of life that longs to be.

For in the wreckage, hope rebloom,
From silent nights, new flowers plume.
Through every tear, a spark ignites,
In vivid hues, the heart delights.

Resilient Whispers from the Ashes

From embered past, soft voices rise,
In whispered strength, the spirit flies.
Through charred remains, new paths emerge,
In every loss, the heart will surge.

The ashes cradle stories lost,
Yet from the flames, we count the cost.
With each new dawn, the past is shed,
In shadows deep, fresh dreams are bred.

In warmth of fire, we find our way,
The light restored at break of day.
Resilient tales, like phoenix soar,
From broken ground, they rise once more.

These whispers, frail yet full of grace,
Speak of the courage time can trace.
In every heartbeat, echoes call,
Reminders sweet, we can stand tall.

For from the ashes, life will bloom,
In tender hearts, there's room for room.
In flames we forge, in trials we trust,
In whispers low, we rise from dust.

Blossoms Amidst the Cinders

In cinders gray, a dream takes flight,
With every bloom, a spark ignites.
Through crackled ground, the colors break,
In tender hues, the world shall wake.

Soft petals kiss the scorched terrain,
Resilient hearts defy the pain.
With every breath, we paint anew,
Life's vibrant shades, a wondrous view.

A vision bright in twilight's glow,
The past may burn, yet we still grow.
In gardens where the memories lie,
We weave the dreams that once did fly.

With fragrant whispers in the air,
The blossoms rise, a silent prayer.
In trials faced, we find our song,
Together, we shall all grow strong.

From ashes dark, we craft our way,
In every night, we seek the day.
In blooms of hope, our hearts will find,
The beauty lies in love entwined.

Shadows of Metamorphosis

In the twilight, whispers roam,
Specters dance in a twilight dome.
Leaves of dusk fall like dreams,
Shattered hope, or so it seems.

With each shadow, secrets wane,
A ghostly breeze through fallen rain.
Transforming hearts, we dare to chase,
The truth buried in time and space.

As the sun yields to the night,
Rebirth stirs in gentle flight.
From ashes cold, a spark ignites,
Revealing paths to wondrous sights.

In corners dark, desire grows,
In hidden depths, a river flows.
A change awaits, though we may fear,
Hope's melody for those who hear.

Through labyrinths of fate we tread,
Each step forward, new life bred.
Embrace the shadows, don't retreat,
For in their depths, our souls shall meet.

Tracing the Arc of Flame

Flickering sparks in the night sky,
A touch of warmth as shadows fly.
Wings of fire, they weave and soar,
Unraveling tales forevermore.

Each glow a promise, fierce and bright,
A dance of destiny in the light.
The flame may flicker, dim, or fade,
Yet in its heart, ambitions laid.

Tracing arcs through the darkness deep,
In embers' glow our visions creep.
To soar higher, we press ahead,
Fueled by whispers of dreams long dead.

When flames collide and ashes blend,
From the chaos, new paths we send.
A journey carved in smoke and dust,
In the fire's heart, we find our trust.

As night descends and shadows loom,
We bear the weight of our own doom.
Yet still, we rise from crackling flames,
Chasing the echoes of our names.

Growth Cradled in Heat

In the warmth of earth, seeds lie low,
Awaiting rains in a gentle flow.
Amidst the silence, life unfolds,
A tale of courage, quiet and bold.

Beneath the sun's benevolent gaze,
Nature whispers in verdant ways.
From humble roots to lofty trees,
Hearts awaken, guided by the breeze.

Cradled in heat, potential stirs,
Every leaf a story, each branch furthers.
Through trials faced and storms endured,
Life's tenacity, forever assured.

In fields of green and blooms of gold,
The cycle continues, endlessly told.
With every dawn, new colors rise,
Painting hope across the skies.

So let us bloom where we are sown,
With every heart, our strength has grown.
In the cradle of warmth, we bloom,
Embracing light, dispelling gloom.

Resurgence in the Ashen Depths

From embered remains of what once was,
Resilience stirs, igniting applause.
Emerging soft from shadows cast,
Life whispers gently, cementing the past.

In ashen depths, dreams linger on,
Transforming night into a dawn.
With every breath, we forge and mend,
The cycle of loss, a precious friend.

Rebirth unfolds in quiet grace,
Among the ruins, a sacred space.
With roots entwined in stories old,
New chapters waiting to be told.

Through trials faced, the spirit thrives,
In every heartbeat, courage strives.
From shattered layers, life ascends,
In the tapestry of time, we blend.

For in the depths, our strength resides,
In every tear, a lesson hides.
Resurgence born from ashes sown,
A symphony of life, fully grown.

The Fusion of Fire and Life

In the heart where flames entwine,
Life dances bright, a spark divine.
With every flicker, tales emerge,
A passion born from heat's surge.

Together they collide and soar,
Elemental forces, evermore.
Bound in warmth, where shadows fall,
A tapestry of life we call.

Embers whisper through the night,
Carrying dreams held out of sight.
In this realm where spirits flow,
Hope ignites; together, we grow.

Through the ashes, seeds take flight,
Nurtured by the radiant light.
The fire guides the wandering heart,
Through every end, a brand new start.

In every blaze, a story spun,
Threads of courage, the battle won.
For life and fire, hand in hand,
Will teach us to forever stand.

Unfolding Within the Blaze

Within the blaze, a secret stirs,
A whispered tale in flickered blurs.
Each flame a portal, bright and bold,
Revealing treasures, stories told.

Roots extend beneath the flame,
Their strength and faith will guide the same.
Like vines entwined, they grasp the light,
Unfolding dreams within the night.

The warmth wraps round like a cherished song,
In the flicker, we all belong.
A tapestry of scars and grace,
Unfolding life, in fire's embrace.

Moments rise and twist like smoke,
With every breath, the silence spoke.
In the dance of ember's glow,
A world alive, where passions flow.

From ashes, wisdom softly sings,
Of courage found in fragile things.
For within the blaze, we ignite,
The heart of life, fierce and bright.

Roots of Courage in the Ember

In quiet embers, strength is born,
Where shadows linger, hope is worn.
Roots reach deep in scorched terrain,
Through every challenge, love will reign.

Courage blooms in the silent night,
Nurtured gently by flickering light.
A heartbeat strong beneath the ash,
In the warmth, the spirits clash.

Every crackle, a promise made,
Together, fear and doubt will fade.
Through the heat of trials endured,
New paths arise, our hearts assured.

In glowing circles, hope's embrace,
Ignites the strength that time won't erase.
For roots that tremble, shake, and bend,
Will rise again; they will not end.

So in the ember's tender light,
Let courage blossom, pure and bright.
For from the depths of smoky haze,
The heart will soar through fiery days.

Spiral Dance of Resilience

In the spiral dance, we learn to bend,
Through every twist, a new ascend.
Against the wind, we spin and sway,
Resilience blooms, come what may.

The flames ignite our grounded roots,
In fiery arches, courage shoots.
With life's rhythm, we find our way,
A symphony anew each day.

As shadows flicker, hearts ignite,
We rise together in shared light.
Through challenges that life bestows,
The spiral carries us as we grow.

Embrace the dance, let spirits sing,
As hope unfurls on resilient wings.
In every rise and every fall,
We create the magic, hear the call.

Together, in the swirling blaze,
We forge our paths, unbound by maze.
In the spiral dance, forever free,
Resilience blooms; it's meant to be.

The Fire's Tender Embrace of Life

In the heart of the wood, a flicker ignites,
Whispers of warmth chase away the night.
Crimson tendrils beckon with grace,
Life's fragile dance in a fiery embrace.

Beneath the folds of the burning light,
Dreams are formed, taking flight.
Amber and gold weave tales so fine,
In each crackle, the world intertwines.

The bravest blooms push forth with pride,
From ashes, they rise, undeterred by the tide.
Fire's kiss, a gentle caress,
Nurtures the seeds of eagerness.

In the blaze, shadows twist and weave,
A tapestry born of hope and believe.
Gathered warmth in the cool of the eve,
Life's pulse echoes, urging to achieve.

And thus in flames, the cycle returns,
With flickering breath, the spirit learns.
Life forged anew, in fire's embrace,
A symphony of light in a sacred space.

Twisted Sprouts of Rebirth

From the remnants of silence, a sprout breaks free,
Twisting and turning, full of glee.
Nature's own magic, a subtle art,
In each tender shoot lies a beating heart.

From forgotten soil, whispers arise,
Encouraged by sun and tender skies.
Roots intertwine in a secret ballet,
Life's joyous return in a brilliant display.

The world holds its breath as green unfurls,
Promises of beauty in delicate whirls.
Each leaf a story, a tale to weave,
Of strength and hope for all who believe.

In hidden corners, the songbirds sing,
Of treasures bestowed by the coming spring.
Embraced by the light, the earth calls forth,
Twisted sprouts of rebirth, a joyful worth.

Among the shadows, bright visions bloom,
In the dance of life, there's always room.
Nature's embrace, in cycles so sweet,
Every ending, a promise, a new heartbeat.

A Dance of Resilient Tendrils

In a world of whispers, the vines entwine,
Each tendril reaching, in rhythm divine.
A dance of resilience, they sway and bend,
Through tempests and trials, they never end.

With courage rooted in the deepest ground,
In every heartbeat, nature's sound.
Veils of green unspool beneath the sky,
Tendrils resilient, together they fly.

Twisting and turning, they seek the light,
Embracing the shadows of long, lonely nights.
Their whispers a promise of days to come,
The dance continues, a steady drum.

Each leaf a testament to what will thrive,
Amidst all dangers, they strive, they strive.
Emerging from silence where dreams seem frail,
Their dance is a story, of hope, a tale.

In the garden of life, they'll flourish and grow,
With tendrils entwined in a radiant flow.
Amongst the chaos, they'll write their song,
A dance of resilient tendrils, ever strong.

The Secrets Beneath the Embered Ash

In the quiet stillness of embered ash,
Lies the memory of moments, a fleeting flash.
Whispers of secrets in the soot remain,
Echoes of life beneath sorrow's stain.

Beneath the surface, the embers glow,
Stories of strength hidden, yet aglow.
From charred remains, fresh dreams ignite,
In the canvas of night, revealing their light.

Every flicker a promise, every spark a tale,
Of resilience born when the old must pale.
In shadows of grief, hope threads anew,
The secrets of past that the fire once grew.

Embers dance lightly, a waltz through the dark,
Glimmers of wisdom, an ancient mark.
In the heart of decay, renewal takes flight,
From embered ash, a world bathed in light.

With patience and grace, the earth shall reclaim,
The beauty from sorrow, a patient flame.
For beneath the ashes, a spark holds the key,
To secrets of life, eternally free.

Knots of Life After Destruction

In shadows cast by shattering light,
Where dreams were lost in endless night,
A whisper stirs, a budding thrill,
In heartbeats soft, new hopes instill.

The tangled mess of fading past,
Weaves tales of growth that hold steadfast,
Each knot a bond, each tear a thread,
To weave anew where once we bled.

From ash and dust, resilience sings,
A phoenix flown on vibrant wings,
Through storm and doubt, the spirit climbs,
With every breath, the rapture rhymes.

With hands entwined and laughter bright,
In gardens grown from ancient plight,
Life knits a tapestry so grand,
A legacy, hand in hand.

So let the winds of change embrace,
And guide us to a vibrant place,
Where knots of life entwine and glow,
In patterns rich, forever grow.

Emergence from the Cinders

From cinders cold, a glow so bright,
A flicker bold in darkest night,
With every spark, a story spun,
Of battles lost and victories won.

The charred remains of what has been,
Hold secrets wrapped in ashen skin,
Yet from the depths, a voice does rise,
A chorus strong beneath the skies.

Each ember whispers tales of yore,
Of broken hearts that dared to soar,
In whispered winds, resilience found,
Through open wounds, new hopes unbound.

Beneath the soil, in shadows sown,
Life's tapestry intricately grown,
From scorched beginnings, fragile threads,
A fabric rich where courage spreads.

So let the flames of trial dance,
Embrace the chaos, dare the chance,
From cinders grey, we rise anew,
Emergence strong, and ever true.

Roots Entwined with Embers

In twilight's hush where dark meets light,
Root systems weave out of sight,
Entwined with embers, fierce and bold,
A legacy of warmth retold.

Together deep, they burrow down,
In harmony, the earth's rich crown,
The scars of fire not lost, but grown,
In whispers soft, the seed is sown.

With every struggle comes a change,
A dance of life, both vast and strange,
Embers glow where shadows merge,
An ancient song, the roots converge.

In tangled dance beneath the ground,
Bound spirits rise, where love is found,
Among the ruins, life abounds,
In unity, new strength resounds.

So cherish bonds that fire ignites,
For life emerges from its fights,
With roots entwined, we find our grace,
In fiery hearts, we embrace space.

A Symphony of Scorched Growth

A symphony in whispering winds,
Where nature's song of healing begins,
Each note a tale of ash and blaze,
In melodies of shifting days.

From crater deep, new melodies play,
Resilient hearts find brighter day,
With scorched terrain, the blooms arise,
In vibrant hues beneath the skies.

The rhythm beats in earthy grace,
As life finds path through scarred embrace,
Where echoes of the past resound,
In every stride, new hope is found.

With branches reaching, strong and wide,
Beneath the sun, we turn the tide,
In every heartbeat, life does swell,
A symphony the forest tells.

So let the scars be songs we share,
With harmonies beyond compare,
In nature's arms, we find our way,
A symphony of hope, we play.

2034

How AI Changed Humanity Forever

spark

PREFACE

A Story of Change

In a world where the improbable becomes the everyday, the future is only limited by the bounds of our imagination.

A Story of Change

When ChatGPT was introduced in late 2022, it captured the world's imagination.

2034 is about the decade that followed, when humans changed the world. With AI.

Written in the year 2024, *2034* is a speculative nonfiction book that offers bold predictions of what happened to the world, told from the perspective of the future looking back at how humanity changed with artificial intelligence.

Ten years might seem like a short period; however, it will prove to be the defining decade in our relationship with AI. Like any new partnership, it will involve the "norming and storming" phases of learning how to co-exist. The early phases of any new relationship are both beautiful and challenging, as partners decide how to show up for each other, what to rely on the other for, and what to do for themselves as individuals.

2034 is a story that captures the breadth and depth of this relationship between humanity and AI, highlighting moments of harmony, conflict, and everything in between. It is clear to many that AI will be a highly disruptive technology, more so than even the internet or the smartphone. In the face of this disruption, the choice everyone has to make is to either be disrupted *by* AI or to be disruptive *with* AI.

2034 is a story of those who chose to lead the disruption and how they thrived. It is also a story of those who unknowingly chose to be disrupted by AI and how they got left behind. When AI first started to appear in visible ways and show signs it could carry out tasks previously thought to be uniquely human, the debate quickly turned to "human vs. AI." However, this "human vs. AI" paradigm evolved to "human + AI" by 2034.

2034 is a story of how, once we got over our initial fears of being replaced by AI, we began to see the potential of using AI to build the world we wanted.

This reflection of how AI changed humanity, written from the perspective of the future, is not to make predictions of what may or may not happen. Many of the ideas presented in *2034* are intentionally not realistic: they are designed to provoke you, the reader, to reflect.

As you read this story, observe your reactions to the ideas and take them as a prompt to reflect more deeply about your openness to change. Does the idea of change frighten you? Or does it excite you?

2034 invites your imagination to run free, unlimited and unconstrained by reality. Dream, imagine, and construct in your mind possible realities, and then enjoy playing within them. This story is a safe space to become curious about the future. About our future.

This is a story of the next phase of human evolution, not of the evolution of AI.

2034 is a story of how AI came into our lives and how, as result, humans changed.

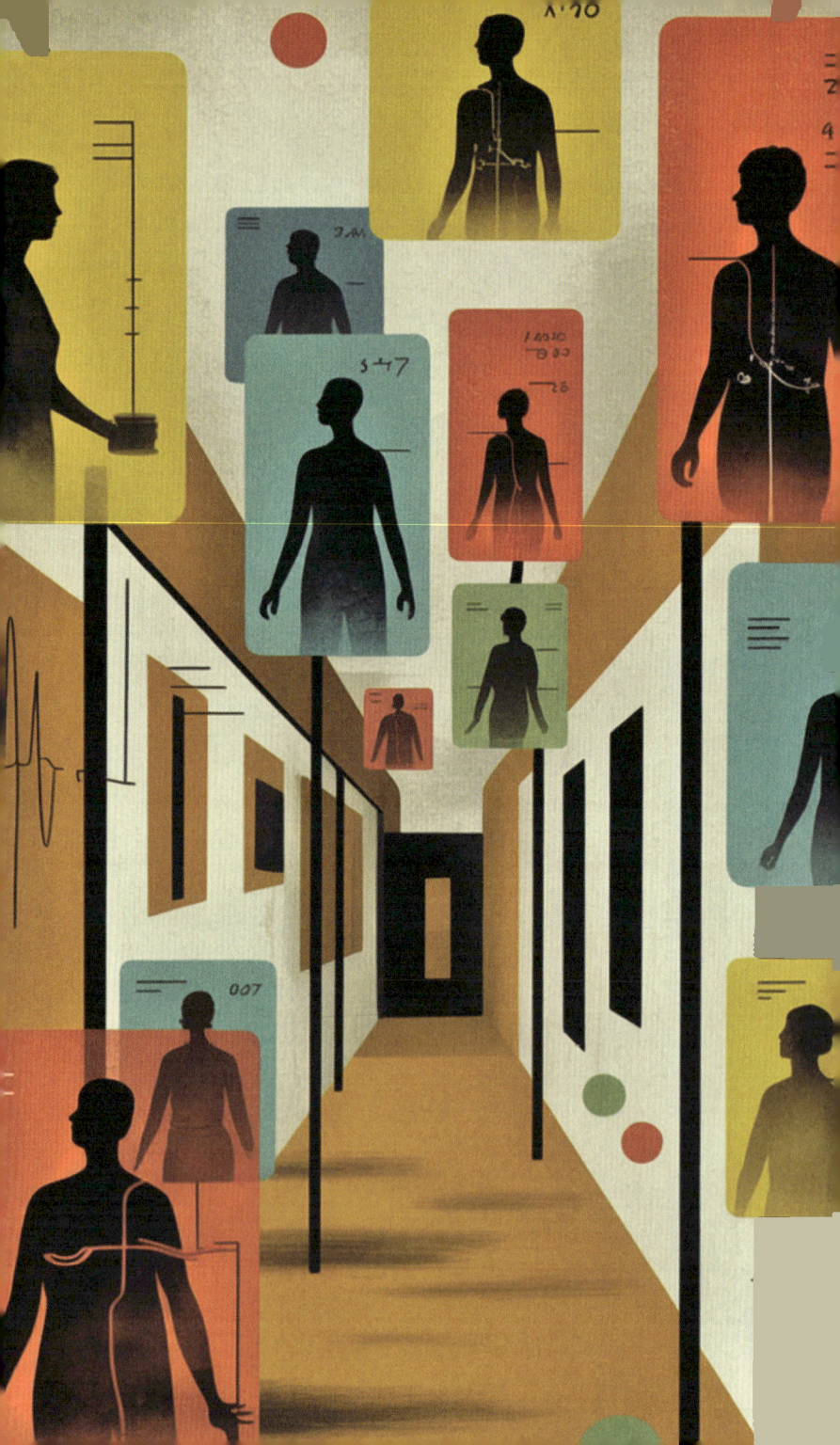

ARRIVE

The Great Pivot

The mind's gifts are not bound by the
ordinary; in every gaze, a universe of
possibilities unfolds.

The Great Pivot

January 1, 2034.

As I look out my window, I see a busy street corner. A woman chats with her smart earrings, checking the likelihood of rain. A teenager laughs at a joke shared by his AI wristband. A child asks her toy, now doubling as an educational tool, why the sky is blue. It is hard to imagine a world without these interactions, which have now become the norm in 2034.

Today's reality is starkly different from life a decade ago.

Back in 2024, people fumbled with outdated devices and asked simple questions to virtual voice assistants that often produced answers that made little sense. It was a world where face-to-face conversations were more common than AI written text messages and AI summarized emails. Handwritten letters, postcards, and poems still carried emotions more profound than any emoji could convey. Busy city streets buzzed with chatter, not the hum of drones. Decisions were made more from human intuition and less from algorithm-driven predictions.

This world wasn't AI deprived. It was just simpler.

Screens didn't predict what you wanted to see next. Autonomous assistants didn't finish tasks for you without your involvement. Human connections were strengthened by shared experiences and memories, not synchronized cloud data.

People were quick to judge and even quicker to dismiss AI back in 2024. Some even took pride in not having to rely on AI. Society was scared, sensing it was on the brink of profound change, but still clinging to its old ways.

The initial introduction of AI to consumers through rudimentary tools like ChatGPT turned out to be only the trailer for the movie. We became intrigued with the two-minute trailer, finding novel and fun applications that temporarily amused us. Having ChatGPT tell a joke, write a poem, or proofread a student's assignment were fairly benign applications of the technology. However, in the years that followed, the feature-length movie was released, and we were no longer playing with the trailer anymore. And that is when AI changed the world, forever.

The past decade is what we now refer to as *The Great Pivot*.

From the year 2024 to the year 2034, the world pivoted to integrate AI in nearly everything, from developing art, to writing essays, to analyzing data, to making decisions, to automating processes, to discovering new materials, to organizing our world, and much, much more.

In the year 2024, the world without the internet was unimaginable. Similarly, by the year 2034, the world is now unimaginable without AI. This period was *The Great Pivot*.

The Great Pivot was a time when imaginations became limitless, and possibilities seemed endless. The lines between what was real and what was possible began to blur. With constraints lifted, we began to dream again, and many of those dreams came true. It has arguably been the most exciting time to be alive and part of our world.

Our relationship with AI is nothing short of a love affair. We love the magic that AI still delivers for our minds. Machines generate soul-stirring art and code that has changed our lives in unimaginable ways. Each morning feels like Christmas, with new presents being delivered to our doorstep.

But like any love story, it is not without its dark side.

Beneath the surface admiration, there have been storms filled with fears. One such storm was a modern-day revolution when entire communities chose to disconnect and live a life untouched by AI. As these communities emerged, from New York to London to Sydney, they became safe zones for those struggling with the speed of change.

Amid these storms, the most inspiring solutions often came from the unlikeliest source: children. Young people, buried in voice-driven manuals, would guide their grandparents through recalibrating their home AI systems. Schoolyards were filled with chatter, not just of the latest AI games, but also of AI hacks. It was often the youngest feet that led the way for the rest of us.

History isn't a series of events that took place long ago. History is a living, breathing collection of emotions, experiences, and lessons. History is about reflecting on how these moments made us laugh, cry, ponder, and sometimes rebel. Each tale is a reflection on how we grew and evolved.

It's timely to pause and reflect on *The Great Pivot* and how AI changed humanity forever during this past decade. Specifically how we changed humanity by using AI.

Welcome to 2034.

COMPILED

AI Took My Job

When the unexpected comes knocking at your door, it's a reminder that life is full of surprises waiting to be explored.

AI Took My Job

Humans have always been innovators.

Think about the first time a train ever left a station, or when the first light bulb lit up a room. Every one of those moments changed how we lived forever.

Earlier inventions made our work easier or faster. Like washing machines that cleaned our clothes without us having to scrub, or electronic calculators that did math without us having to use a pen and paper.

AI went beyond making our work easier and faster, though. It started doing things we hadn't even thought of, in ways we couldn't have imagined.

At first, AI was widely used for efficiency, as it could write, analyze, research, and create faster than humans. Then it was used for effectiveness, as AI could do so many things better than humans. And that's when everything changed, forever.

This brought a new word to our world: "*compiled*." At first, this word sounded weird and techie. But with time, the public understood what it meant.

Compiled wasn't about machines taking over human jobs. It was also about machines doing things in ways that went beyond human capabilities. It was a whole new level of change that we had to learn to deal with. *Compiled* showed us that, as it turns out, many human jobs can in fact be reduced to algorithms and code—and that humans are not as unique as was once believed.

A Humbling of Humanity

For centuries, humans took great pride in our creativity, shown through art, architecture, literature, and science. We painted the Sistine Chapel, wrote Pride and Prejudice, and decoded DNA. Every accomplishment boosted the human ego, making us believe we were the kings and queens of capability and creativity.

And then AI entered the scene. The initial assumption was that machines might take over simple, repetitive tasks but never tasks that involved "uniquely human" skills. We believed that creativity, emotions, and deep thinking were only born out of the human soul, and inspired only from human experiences. We were wrong.

In 2028, when *Joyful*, not a human but an AI model, was awarded the Nobel Prize in Literature, we all watched with awe to see a collection of code celebrated for its ability to create narratives. An AI model had created stories that resonated more deeply, with more people than many human authors ever had.

Trained on a vast array of literary works and cultural texts, *Joyful* could stitch together narratives that were intimately relevant to individual readers globally. *Joyful*'s ability to analyze and understand the intricacies of human emotions and cultural context led to the creation of stories that were not just universally appealing but that felt deeply personal.

Instead of literature being relevant to only a certain age demographic, gender group, socioeconomic subclass, or cultural background, *Joyful* paved the way for universally relevant literature that was nuanced enough to appeal to literally everyone. This brought a new era of literature that was inclusive and respectful of the culturally diverse backgrounds across the planet, which now has over 10 billion humans in the year 2034.

This was a departure from traditional literature, which, despite its best efforts, often had the unconscious biases and limitations of its human authors reflected in it. Adoption of this new style of literature was also accelerated by the decline of human authors, who kept getting canceled by society for offending some subsegment of the population. It became a liability for human authors to publish literature for fear of reputational harm. Society was so quick to go after human authors for including the wrong sentence in their works that human authors stopped publishing new works altogether. AI models have now become the primary source of literature – a situation of our own making.

As human authors got *compiled,* it sparked debates about the essence of creativity and the value of human experience in literature. While a few were upset by the loss of the human touch in storytelling, many argued that AI models like *Joyful* were simply the next step in the evolution of literature, free from the biases, stereotypes, and limitations of human authors. The publishing industry, once hesitant to embrace AI authors, quickly adapted to this new reality, recognizing the commercial viability and global appeal of AI-generated works.

In this new era, some human authors found niches in providing the raw emotional and experiential inputs that fed AI models like *Joyful,* while other human authors focused on critique and interpretation, offering human perspectives on AI-generated literature. This duo of human creativity and AI efficiency became the new norm in the literary world. Humanity's self-confidence about its own intellectual and creative superiority suffered, blow after blow, with the adoption of AI, which humanity itself had created. It has been a period of great humility for humanity.

A Transfer of Wealth

One of the most chaotic changes of the past decade came in 2029.

Public financial markets, often driven by human speculation and emotion, were turned upside down forever. *GreenRock*, an AI-driven forecasting system, began predicting stock market moves with an accuracy that had never been seen before. An algorithm began deciding the changes of stock prices through its automated and systematic trading activity. Stock markets everywhere soared and plummeted, based on *GreenRock*'s forecasts.

Fortunes were made and lost within minutes. We are still grappling with the realities of this new economic order, as *GreenRock* marked the beginning of the end of public stock markets. Smaller companies quickly began to delist themselves from the stock exchanges, unable to cope with the ungrounded fluctuations in their companies' market capitalization.

Back in 2024, there were nearly 50,000 companies listed across all the public stock markets globally. By 2034, that number has come down to under 30,000. The number of public companies is believed to have peaked, as we continue to see the decline accelerate. Many of the largest public companies have announced their intention to delist from stock markets in the coming years, turning the public markets into a litter tray for the less desired.

This change is impacting how wealth is created and distributed. Ownership in companies is now returning to large investors and investment funds. For everyday people, instead of owning stocks, they now own shares in private investment funds, who then buy shares in large private companies. The liquidity of investments has dried up, meaning that investors can't buy or sell their private company shares as easily. This is forcing more investor due diligence in advance, knowing their investments will be locked up for longer, in contrast to the good old days of being able to buy and sell public stocks in real time from your phone.

It also has meant less leverage within the financial system. Given the lack of liquidity of private share ownership, banks are not able to lend as much money to investors. With less leverage in the system, there is less investment, and economic activity has already started to slow. Private companies can choose who they want as shareholders and, more importantly, who they don't. This has given more power to the management and boards of companies than previous times, and forced investors to be on good behavior.

Compensation at previously public companies has also gone through huge upheaval. Stock-based compensation plans, which were generally liquid and, therefore, as good as cash, are no longer desirable for employees. They now demand cash compensation instead. This has reduced the profitability of companies; however, has increased tax revenues for governments, as employment income is taxed at higher rates.

Transparency of company performance also also changed—one of the benefits of being private versus public. Without the requirement for quarterly reporting and being subject to the short-sightedness of public markets, private companies have increased investment in longer-term initiatives and have started to take on more risk.

Greenrock compiling public stock markets turned out to be a democratizing force for the greater good, as the financial system is now less easy for those with money and power to control and manipulate for their benefit.

A Reconstruction of Spaces

The AI-driven company *Remake* made waves back in 2030. Architecture, we had formerly believed, was a combination of human creativity and engineering. But *Remake* began designing buildings and structures that were not only beautiful but more efficient, sustainable, and safer than anything humans had come up with previously. It would consider factors like local climate, cultural nuances, and material strength in ways human engineers hadn't or couldn't. Cities began to transform from boring concrete jungles into art museums, thanks to *Remake.*

The physical reconstruction of our cities has begun, inspired by a better, more sustainable and more affordable way forward.

Each structure designed by *Remake* reflected the cultural heritage and history of its location, using AI to analyze historical patterns and local artistic themes, thereby creating buildings that are not only physically but also culturally part of their environment.

In Marrakech, *Remake* developed a new social housing complex that was a modern interpretation of the traditional Riad. The structure featured a central courtyard—a quintessential element of Moroccan architecture—providing a communal and cooling open space. The building's façade was covered with geometric patterns and mosaics inspired by Islamic art, with a color palette reflecting the reds and greens typical of Marrakech's cityscape. *Remake* also integrated sustainable features informed by traditional methods, such as thick walls for natural insulation and water features for cooling, demonstrating a blend of cultural respect with environmental consciousness.

In New Orleans, *Remake*'s designs seamlessly integrated into the city's historic fabric. The AI developed a series of mixed-use buildings in the French Quarter that resonated with the city's Creole and French influences. These structures adapted iconic elements, such as wrought-iron balconies, pastel-colored façades, and verdant courtyards. For example, the balconies were designed with smart, adaptive materials that could change configuration to optimize sunlight and airflow, enhancing energy efficiency. Inside, the buildings were equipped with advanced acoustics technology, a nod to New Orleans' musical heritage, creating spaces ideal for live jazz performances.

Buildings designed by *Remake* are "smart" from inception, integrated with IoT (Internet of Things) devices for energy management, climate control, and even resident health monitoring, leading to more efficient and responsive living spaces. *Remake* pushed the boundaries for using new materials, like self-healing concrete or pollution-absorbing exterior walls. Its designs incorporated recycled materials that reduced waste and environmental impact.

Looking back, *Remake compiled* much of the traditional construction and architecture industry for the better. Its cost-effective and efficient designs lowered the time required for construction and renovation, helping alleviate housing crises in many urban areas. This is also leading to more diverse and vibrant communities.

Remake was an example of how AI not only made a traditional industry more efficient, but also more effective.

A Humancare System

Ripe for disruption, the healthcare system of the past that centered on symptom management was replaced with a humancare system that has altered our understanding of medicine, health, and wellbeing. Where once the halls of hospitals were full of countless medical staff, they now have AI systems, seamlessly orchestrating every aspect of humancare. *Healix* emerged in 2027 and combined two critical aspects of humancare: diagnostics and personalized medicine. Through its advanced algorithms, *Healix* pioneered a new era where healthcare evolved from a service to a personalized experience, tailored to an individual's genetic blueprint.

Their first major breakthrough was a diagnostic tool capable of detecting early-stage cancer with unprecedented accuracy. Utilizing advanced imaging analysis and a database of millions of pathology reports, *Healix* identified patterns invisible to human doctors. For instance, a patient undergoing a routine scan was alerted to early-stage lung cancer, which *Healix* detected through subtle nodular changes, leading to early intervention and successful treatment. Leveraging heart imaging and real-time health data, *Healix*'s algorithms predicted cardiac events, such as heart attacks, before any physical symptoms were evident. This predictive capability allowed for preemptive medical interventions, drastically reducing the incidence of acute cardiac events.

Healix's approach involved creating detailed genetic profiles of patients. This data, combined with AI analysis, informed the development of customized treatment plans. For example, when a patient with a specific genetic variant finds their standard medication ineffective, *Healix* recommends an alternative drug that uses AI prediction to forecast its effectiveness on a personalized basis. By analyzing how different genetic markers interact with various medications, the efficiency of such recommendations improves and side effects are significantly minimized. Core to *Healix*'s effectiveness is a wearable device that continuously monitors patients' health data. This real-time monitoring allows for dynamic adjustments in treatment plans. A diabetic patient, for instance, receives insulin dosage adjustments based on real-time glucose monitoring and AI analysis.

The traditional healthcare system has been *compiled* by companies like *Healix*. It feels naïve now to think that we used to expect a human doctor to be able to diagnose, treat, and monitor patients with minimal technology.

The doctors who didn't adopt services like *Healix* though have been *compiled*, as the bar is now higher from patients due for their personalized humancare experience. In this new era, the role of human medical professionals has transformed. Doctors, nurses, and pharmacists shifted from being primary caregivers to collaborators with AI, focusing on patient relationship and care management, areas where the human touch remains important.

Medical schools are now teaching students how AI systems work, and recent graduates are not joining hospitals but health-tech conglomerates, where they can contribute towards AI system development and, consequently, have a greater impact on more people.

A Warning of Resistance

Like any other transformative chapter in human history, AI has had its champions and its detractors in the past decade. People were divided into those who saw the potential and aligned themselves with AI and those who, out of fear or pride, chose to stand firm against AI.

One of the defining success stories of the era was *Kova*. Founded as a modest tech company, it wasn't known for anything special until 2025. That year, its leadership initiated an ambitious project where every employee underwent extensive AI-integration training. This wasn't just about using AI tools; it was about synthesizing human intuition with machine efficiency and effectiveness.

The result? Within a year, their productivity surged. They were outperforming their larger, more established competitors and defining a new standard.

Kova didn't disclose how they were using AI. Their LinkedIn page showed an inflated number of employees, because the company realized that if clients knew how small they were, they wouldn't be taken seriously. The company didn't hire a single new employee for years. They didn't need any more people, as their current team continued to get more and more productive, thanks to going all-in on AI.

Kova implemented AI for project management, which not only scheduled tasks but also predicted potential bottlenecks and suggested optimal resource allocation. The company utilized AI for analyzing vast amounts of data, which generated insights that would typically take days of human analysis. These systems provided real-time market trends, customer preferences, and operational efficiencies, enabling rapid and informed decision-making.

For product development, *Kova* used AI to create virtual models and run simulations, drastically reducing the time and cost of prototyping. This allowed for rapid experimentation and iteration.

Kova became synonymous with "less is more," a philosophy that encouraged companies, big and small, to do more with less and see the value in staying small and nimble, versus big and bloated.

By stark contrast stood *Lodafone*.

Lodafone had been a titan in the global telecommunications industry. Its leadership prided themselves on human-centric solutions, asserting that real innovation came from people, not algorithms. Even as AI started to rewrite business rules, *Lodafone* dug its heels in, launching massive campaigns emphasizing the "human touch" in their services. Their flagship stores had large banners declaring, "Real People, Real Connections."

While *Lodafone* emphasized the "human touch" in customer service, they struggled with long wait times and inconsistent service quality. In contrast, competitors using AI chatbots and automated systems provided instant, 24/7 customer support, leading to higher customer satisfaction.

Lodafone's manual network optimizations couldn't match the dynamic, AI-driven optimizations of competitors, resulting in poorer service quality and higher costs. Furthermore, its marketing campaigns, though human-crafted, lacked the personalized touch. They failed to compete with AI-driven targeted advertising and content personalization that rivals used, leading to less effective customer engagement and lower return on investment for their advertising spend.

As 2028 rolled around, their resistance became their downfall. Customers, having tasted the efficiency offered by AI-driven competitors, migrated away. *Lodafone*'s quarterly earnings showed a steep decline, their stock plummeted, and their brand, once a symbol of trust and reliability, started to appear outdated.

By 2031, *Lodafone*, which once boasted a global customer base in the billions, was *compiled* and forced into bankruptcy. Its decline served as a warning: in an era of evolution, adaptation is essential. Those who resisted, no matter how noble their intentions, were left behind in the wake of progress.

A Human Upgrade

In the early 2020s, everyone was becoming a coach—be it a business coach, life coach, or spiritual coach—however by the early 2030s, the new trend was to become a *Life-Crafter*.

As AI handles more mundane and repetitive tasks, humans find themselves with more time and freedom to explore passions and hobbies. *LifeCrafters* help people find, nurture, and monetize these passions. They are modern-day career counselors, guiding people towards fulfilling pursuits, often blending technology and creativity.

For example, a *LifeCrafter* assisted a bank manager in discovering a talent for landscape photography, guiding her to turn this passion into a profitable online business. Another *LifeCrafter* guided an amateur chef in creating a viral food blog and YouTube channel, transforming his culinary hobby into a lucrative influencer career.

They also connect individuals with similar interests, creating communities and networks. For example, a *LifeCrafter* organized a local meetup for drone enthusiasts, leading to collaborative projects and shared learning experiences.

They stay abreast of the latest trends and technologies, advising clients on how to remain relevant and competitive. One *LifeCrafter* introduced a musician to AI-assisted composition tools, helping him create groundbreaking music that resonated with audiences.

The need for purpose and meaning remains a core human need and with much of the human workforce having been *compiled* over the past decade, the search for new pursuits has become increasingly important.

The past decade also changed our understanding of work and value. Previously, value was associated with hours spent, tasks completed, or targets achieved. But in an age when machines outperform humans in all of these metrics, we are redefining what we place a premium on— that bar is much higher now.

The job market saw a surge in roles like *AI Whisperers*, who ensure that AI systems make decisions that are in line with human values, and *Bot Buddies*, who are experts in ensuring seamless synergy between person and machine.

AI's entry into the workspace wasn't about replacement but augmentation. *Assist*—a wearable device— launched in 2032, exemplifies this. It is a device that workers across various industries use to access real-time insights, suggestions, and data on how to do their job better. A chef can get instant flavor pairing recommendations; a teacher can receive custom learning strategies for each student; and a craftsperson can access advanced design techniques at the flick of a finger.

Doctors and nurses use *Assist* to receive real-time updates on patient vitals, drug interaction alerts, and evidence-based treatment suggestions. Surgeons access 3D anatomical models during procedures, enhancing precision and safety.

Field researchers and environmentalists use *Assist* to get instant analysis of soil, air, and water samples. It also provides them with historical environmental data from the location, aiding in quicker and more accurate field assessments.

Salespersons in retail environments use *Assist* to access customer preferences and purchase history, enabling personalized shopping experiences. It also helps in managing inventory by providing real-time stock updates and reorder alerts.

In sports, *Assist* offers athletes and coaches real-time data on performance metrics, health stats, and technique improvement tips. It also suggests personalized training regimes and recovery methods.

The most important innovations were born not when AI overshadowed humans, but when humans and AI harmoniously partnered. Human creations, be it a heartwarming story or a breathtaking skyscraper, reached new heights and depths when supported by machine precision. This relationship redefined the essence of invention, innovation, and imagination.

Compiled, therefore, now has a new meaning. It is no longer about making humans obsolete but about making them better. The initial fears of being *compiled* were mitigated as humans and AI moved forward, together.

SKILL

How AI Became a Verb

Change is the song of evolution,
sung by those brave enough to
dance to a new rhythm.

How AI Became a Verb

When pop star *Saylor Drift* sang in 2024 about "waiting for her AI to sync before heading out for a drink," most of us chuckled. AI was, after all, just another tech gadget, a noun we associated with algorithms.

Fast forward to 2034, AI is no longer a noun but a verb. As fundamental as learning "to read," "to speak," or "to walk," now the verb "to AI" is critical. You must be able to AI now for survival.

It started subtly. At first, magazines had stories of how readers "AI'd their weekends," turning chores and routines into delightfully optimized experiences. Little did we realize that this wasn't merely tech-savvy lingo; it was the start of a new paradigm.

By 2026, it was hard to find an aspect of life untouched by this verbification. Fashionistas spoke about AI'ing their wardrobe, teachers discussed AI'ing their lessons for students, and architects talked about AI'ing their building designs. We began reimagining activities with AI as a critical part of the process.

As with every major shift, there were skeptics. The popular comic strip *Life Before Verbification* featured characters nostalgically recalling days when AI was "just a noun."

As we know, nostalgia may be comforting, but it rarely stands in the way of progress. In making AI a verb, the world redefined what it meant to live, to experience, and to be.

A New Way to Learn

As we ventured further into the 2020s, the integration of AI into our daily lives moved beyond novelty to necessity, particularly in the realm of education. Worldwide, education systems underwent an overhaul with curriculum reforms that placed a significant emphasis on AI proficiency. Traditional computer classes evolved into AI-integration labs. By the age of nine, children understood the logic of algorithmics. By twelve, they were not merely passive consumers of AI but creators, capable of designing simple AI models.

In elementary schools, a typical day commenced with *Yogai*—a unique blend of yoga and AI. Students, with their bio-wearable devices, synced with the classroom AI for a series of guided mindfulness exercises, tailored to individual emotional bio-feedback signals. High school classrooms buzzed with spirited debates on the rights of sentient AIs, the ethical conundrums posed by advanced AI models, and philosophical inquiries into consciousness.

Even recess transformed into an arena where AI played a pivotal role. Students played augmented reality games developed by their friends. These games were not mere pastimes but intellectual battlegrounds where students created AI strategies to beat their friends' creations.

Perhaps the most impactful change was the introduction of personalized learning. The concept of a universal teaching curriculum became obsolete, replaced by AI tutors customized to meet the unique learning styles and needs of each student. These AI tutors, through analysis of a student's strengths, weaknesses, and learning preferences, optimized content and method in real-time.

Consider *Alex*, a high school student with dyslexia, who often struggled with reading. His AI tutor personalized content into audio formats and used text with dyslexia-friendly fonts and colors. For writing assignments, the tutor provided real-time corrective feedback, making the learning process more inclusive for *Alex*.

In a mixed-ability classroom, pacing can be challenging. Take *Leo* and *Mia*, for instance. *Mia* grasped mathematical concepts quickly, while *Leo* needed more time and reinforcement. Their AI tutor identified these pace differences and adjusted accordingly. *Mia* received advanced problem sets and exploratory projects, while *Leo's* lessons included repeated practice and step-by-step explanations. Both students learned the same material but in ways that matched their individual learning speeds.

The AI tutors constantly analyzed student responses and performance. If a student struggled with a particular algebra concept, the tutor instantly introduced alternative explanations to help her understand. This real-time adaptation ensured that learning hurdles were addressed immediately, preventing long-term gaps.

The traditional methods of teaching history also received an upgrade. Instead of relying solely on textbooks, students now immerse themselves in historical events through VR platforms. This deep immersion allows for a full understanding of events. Students ask questions directly to the avatars of historical figures and engage directly with them. History is now cool again.

Education is no longer a one-size-fits-all model but a diverse, adaptive, and deeply personal experience in 2034.

The shift from standardization to customization in learning not only caters to individual growth but also prepares students for a future where adaptability, creativity, and AI literacy are paramount.

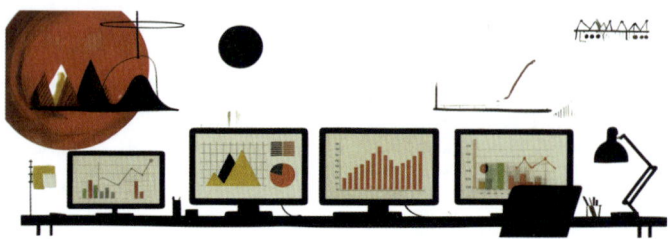

A New Way to Work

In the professional world, the verbification of AI signified a shift in how tasks, decisions, and communication happen. AI ceased to be a mere tool and has become an integral aspect of daily work life, redefining roles, enhancing productivity, and supporting growth.

James, working as a project manager in a construction firm, has seen a big change in his job with the introduction of AI.

Every day, he utilizes AI's predictive analytics to preemptively identify potential project delays or budget issues. The AI system he uses is sophisticated enough to analyze multiple factors simultaneously, from weather patterns affecting construction schedules to supply chain disruptions impacting material availability. It even predicts workforce fluctuations, helping *James* allocate labor resources more efficiently. AI'ing has become an integral part of his workflow, evolving project management from a reactive activity to a proactive discipline.

Sarah's role as a marketing strategist in a retail company has been transformed by AI.

She leverages AI tools to dissect large amounts of consumer data. This data-driven approach allows her to tailor marketing campaigns with a precision that was once unimaginable. She can now target specific audiences with personalized content, ensuring that her campaigns are both creative and highly effective. AI'ing her campaigns means that every decision *Sarah* makes is backed by robust data, leading to increased performance and sales.

In the legal domain, professionals like *David* have experienced a sea change in their approach to research. Gone are the days of poring over legal documents for hours. *David's* AI tools sift through thousands of legal documents rapidly, extracting the relevant case law he needs. *David's* approach in cases is now stronger because he uses insights that only AI can provide, giving him an edge in proceedings. AI'ing his research means that *David* can now focus more on crafting winning arguments and less on the time-consuming process of information gathering.

Kimberly's role as an investment analyst has been enhanced with AI. The AI she uses analyzes global financial data, market trends, and various economic indicators, offering insights that were previously unattainable. This allows *Kimberly* to make well-informed investment recommendations. AI'ing her investment strategies means that she can identify more profitable opportunities and relevant market trends earlier than her competitors. This capability is invaluable in a field where timing and precision are key.

Linda, an entrepreneur, has seamlessly integrated AI into every facet of her business operations. From managing inventory more effectively to enhancing customer service, AI has become a key part of her team. AI tools predict demand patterns, helping *Linda* manage her inventory efficiently, reducing both overstock and sold-out situations. In customer service, AI-driven chatbots handle the majority of issues now. This automation frees up *Linda* and her team to focus on growth projects. By AI'ing her business operations, Linda has not only streamlined processes but also opened up new paths for expansion.

In this new professional era, AI'ing has become synonymous with efficiency and productivity. Whether it is managing complex projects, devising marketing strategies, conducting legal research, analyzing financial markets, or running a business, AI empowers professionals to achieve more with less.

A New Way to Connect

The sweeping influence of AI across generations has brought about a heartwarming trend in community centers around the globe. In these welcoming places, senior citizens are flocking to AI literacy classes, driven by a desire to bridge the ever-widening generational gap and remain a part of their grandchildren's increasingly AI-centric lives.

In a typical session, you might find a 72-year-old grandmother, who initially struggled with the concept of AI, now navigating AI interfaces for video calls, allowing her to connect with her grandchildren in another country. One of the most popular aspects of these classes is the virtual reality segment. Grandparents, who live hours away from their family, learn to participate in shared virtual reality experiences with their grandchildren. These examples reflect a determination of older generations not to be left behind in a rapidly evolving digital world, a world native to their grandchildren.

In the context of modern human relationships, AI has become a valuable mediator, transforming the way we interact and understand each other. The once simple question, "Did you AI that?" has evolved to encompass many meanings, challenging our understanding of empathy, understanding, and connection.

Consider the case of *Emily* and *Mark*, a couple who frequently found themselves entangled in misunderstandings. They turned to an AI relationship assistant, *HarmonAI*, for guidance. *HarmonAI*, equipped with algorithms for personality analysis and conflict resolution, suggested specific communications for them, down to the words to use. For instance, when a disagreement arose about financial planning, *HarmonAI* told *Emily* to approach the conversation with data and facts, resonating with *Mark's* analytical nature, while advising *Mark* to acknowledge the emotional aspects important to *Emily*. The result was a more constructive and empathetic dialogue, leading to mutual understanding and far less conflict.

In the realm of friendship, AI has reimagined social planning. Take the example of a group of college friends. Planning outings used to be a logistical nightmare, with each person's preferences and schedules to consider. They started using an AI social coordinator, *GroupTune*, which analyzed each person's likes, dislikes, and calendar availability to suggest outing ideas that catered to everyone. *GroupTune* proposed a weekend hike when it noticed a shared interest in outdoor activities, clear schedules, good weather and a discount from a tour company. The outings became not only more inclusive but also more enjoyable, as everyone's preferences were considered.

However, this has raised questions about the authenticity of AI-moderated emotions and actions. The AI-assisted apology that *Mark* made to *Emily*, or the AI-planned surprise birthday party *Mark* threw for *Emily*, sparked debates. Was the apology less sincere because *HarmonAI* helped craft it? Did the surprise lose its genuineness because *GroupTune* organized it?

On one hand, AI's assistance in understanding and managing interpersonal dynamics has improved communication and inclusivity. On the other hand, the reliance on AI to navigate the complexities of human emotions and interactions has led some to question the authenticity of these experiences. The charm of human imperfection is lost when AI steps in. However, AI's involvement doesn't necessarily diminish sincerity but rather it enhances our abilities to express and connect.

In recognition of this issue, generative AI platforms began to employ watermarking techniques to distinguish AI-inspired content. Invisible to the naked eye or ear, these watermarks could be detected only by other AIs. This attempt at transparency, however, was short-lived, as market pressures led platforms to create watermark-free content, blurring the lines even further between human and AI creations.

This shift in AI's role in media and relationships became a point of generational divide. For older generations, a clear distinction between human and AI-generated content was critical in maintaining a sense of authenticity. Though younger generations, raised in an AI-saturated environment, saw no issue with AI's role everywhere. To them, whether a conversation was AI-guided or a get-together AI-planned mattered little, as long as the outcome was positive and desirable.

AI, once a mere tool, has now become an integral part in shaping relationships and our understanding of connection.

A New Way to Serve

Public services are meant to serve the public, however in the past decade, massive disruption has happened to the most important public services: healthcare, education, transportation, and infrastructure. This disruption happened at the hands of AI being used by private sector companies. This disruption highlights a stark contrast: while the private sector surged ahead, embracing AI's potential, public systems struggled to keep pace, stuck in bureaucracy and outdated approaches.

The private sector's embrace of AI was enthusiastic and aggressive. Meanwhile, governments and public sectors lagged far behind. The sluggish pace of bureaucracy, constrained budgets, data privacy concerns, and a deep-rooted aversion to change left public services antiquated and inefficient. For example, European nations, once the leaders of public system quality, found their services outdated compared to the dynamic, AI-driven private alternatives. The disparity in service quality, efficiency, and innovation between the public and private sectors became glaringly obvious.

This disparity led to a mass migration of the general population from public to private systems. In healthcare, people turned to private clinics with AI-powered health management, preferring them over the sluggish and impersonal public health services. In education, parents increasingly chose private schools with AI-enhanced learning for their children, leading to a sharp decline in public school enrollments. Public transportation systems, once the backbone of urban mobility, lost commuters to AI-optimized private transport options that offered efficiency, comfort, and personalization.

The public systems, still funded by taxpayer money, became bloated relics of a past era: inefficient, underused, and struggling to justify their relevance. The political landscape began to reflect this shift. Politicians who campaigned on platforms of reducing government size, cutting taxes, and diminishing the role of public systems in favor of private AI-driven solutions started winning elections. Their promises resonated with a population that had already witnessed the benefits of privatized, AI-enhanced services.

As new governments took office, public systems receded further into the background. Attempts to integrate AI into these systems were too little, too late, and often lacked the sophistication and effectiveness of their private counterparts. Public services, once the cornerstone of societal support, were now overshadowed by private entities that offered better, faster, and more personalized services.

This period marked a fundamental shift in the role of government and public systems in several countries that did not "get on the bus." Taxpayers questioned the value of their contributions to systems they no longer used or needed. The AI revolution in the private sector, therefore, changed how services were delivered; it fundamentally altered the expectations of the public sector.

The full domino effect of these changes has yet to be seen but in the coming decade, the role of taxes, public services and even elected officials will continue to come under greater scrutiny. The floodgates are open now for private companies to innovate and bring to the public better, cheaper, and more effective services than governments are able to provide. The erosion of trust in public systems has meant a world changed forever.

A New Way to Inspire

As the divide between the AI literate and the AI illiterate grew, the need to inspire people to learn "to AI" became evident. This meant an inclusive approach to AI training. AI was too powerful, its implications too profound, to be accessible only to a privileged few. Recognizing the urgency of the situation, organizations around the world took decisive action with a wave of programs aimed at fostering AI literacy across diverse demographics, ensuring that no one was left behind.

In South Korea, the ambitious *AI for All* initiative marked the first step towards democratizing AI education. The initiative reached out to marginalized groups and older citizens – demographics often overlooked in tech advancement waves.

For example, a workshop titled "AI Basics for Everyday Life" attracted a diverse group of attendees, from small-business owners looking to integrate AI into their operations, to retirees curious about the new digital world.

It included an online platform, *AI Bridge*, which became particularly popular among young adults and professionals. It featured gamified learning modules, AI simulations, and community forums where learners could interact, share ideas, and collaborate on projects. *AI Bridge* also offered job-matching services, linking skilled individuals with AI-related jobs.

The *AI for All* initiative included mobile learning units that traveled to remote areas, ensuring that geographical limitations did not limit access to AI education. These units were equipped with the latest satellite technology and staffed by skilled educators who brought AI to the doorsteps of those living in remote locations.

AI for All became a model for other countries, showcasing how thoughtful, inclusive, and well-structured programs could effectively bridge the AI literacy gap quickly.

Brazil's *RetrAIning* program, with a fusion of culture and AI education, earned recognition for its approach to bridging the gap. Emphasizing the country's vibrant cultural heritage, the program integrated local arts, music and storytelling, making AI concepts accessible through the celebration of Brazilian identity.

In the colorful streets of Santa Teresa, a project called *AI Art Rio* was launched, where local artists used AI tools to generate intricate patterns and designs for their murals. These murals became visual narratives that told stories of AI's role in society, blending traditional Brazilian storylines with futuristic themes. Walking tours were organized to showcase these AI-infused murals, educating locals and tourists alike about AI in an engaging and visually stunning manner.

In Salvador, known for its musical heritage, *RetrAIning* introduced a project that combined AI with traditional Brazilian music. Musicians and composers collaborated with programmers to create new rhythms and sounds, preserving traditional musical forms while infusing them with modern AI-generated beats.

In a primary school in Fortaleza, children learned basic coding by programming small robots to dance to traditional Brazilian tunes, making the learning process both fun and culturally relevant.

Brazil's approach to AI literacy transcended traditional teaching methods. It celebrated the country's diversity and leveraged it as a tool for engagement. By intertwining AI with the arts, music, and everyday life, *RetrAIning* educated people about AI and enriched Brazilian culture.

The most unexpected development, however, was the formation of the *Horizon* alliance, composed of long-standing big-tech rivals. This alliance aimed to democratize AI knowledge on a global scale.

Horizon was a holistic educational experience. It integrated AI learning with lessons on creativity, ethics, and innovation, ensuring that participants didn't just learn to use AI but also to think and feel with it.

The impact of *Horizon* was felt worldwide. Remote villages in Queensland, where internet access was once a luxury, became hubs of AI learning, with local educators receiving training and resources to teach AI fundamentals.

In the isolated towns of the midwest United States, mobile AI labs brought the latest technology to doorsteps, igniting a spark of enthusiasm. Nairobi's bustling urban centers turned into AI workshops, where young entrepreneurs used AI to solve local problems.

Every individual, regardless of age, location, or background, holds a rightful place in an AI-driven world. The journey to AI literacy is not a privilege, but a shared right for all of humanity.

A New Way to Social Media

The way we interact, share, and experience each other through social platforms was reinvented, creating a completely different digital world. Where there were once a few social media platforms that had billions of users, we now have a sea of niche platforms, each with a stronger sense of identity and community for its users.

Marcus, a musician and songwriter from Germany, experienced this firsthand. He signed up on *HarmonyLink*, a social platform that went beyond surface-level interests. It analyzed *Marcus's* music uploads, his interaction patterns, his musical talent, and his influences to understand his music style.

Thousands of miles away, in Argentina, *Clara*, a seasoned music producer, also signed up for *HarmonyLink*. *Clara* had a knack for blending traditional Latin rhythms with contemporary beats and was on the lookout for fresh talent to collaborate with her.

HarmonyLink suggested a connection between *Marcus* and *Clara* and initiated a collaborative project idea for them. Before *Marcus* and *Clara* even had their first conversation, *HarmonyLink* generated a basic melody combining elements of *Marcus's* songwriting style with *Clara's* production signature. This AI-crafted melody served as a conversation starter. They found themselves discussing their musical journeys, sharing personal experiences, and forming a bond that was as much about friendship as it was about music.

AI also started to forge romantic connections, disrupting the dating app scene. *HeartSync*, an AI-driven matchmaker, entered the scene.

Consider the story of *Sofia* and *Lucas*, two *HeartSync* users from different parts of the world. *Sofia*, a graphic designer from Portugal, was known for her creative spirit and love for adventure. *Lucas*, a Canadian wildlife photographer, shared a similar zest for life and a passion for the arts. Both had tried traditional dating apps but found them lacking in depth.

HeartSync was more sophisticated in its approach. For *Sofia*, the platform recognized her preference for deep, thoughtful conversations over casual chats. It noted her interest in a partner who was creative, and shared her interest in meaningful conservation. The AI picked up on *Lucas's* empathetic nature and his love for storytelling through photography. It identified similarities in their social values, lifestyle choices, and even their sense of humor. *HeartSync* suggested a match between *Sofia* and *Lucas* but the connection did not involve any profiles. *Sofia* and *Lucas* trusted *HeartSync* enough to be immediately connected on a live video call, without knowing anything about each other. As they interacted, both found the conversations flowed effortlessly, as they had to learn about each other by asking questions in real-time versus reading anything in advance.

AI was also being used to clean-up some of the problems that humans had created in online communities.

Ciper was a new type of AI that showed up on existing social platforms. This AI was designed to interact with online bullies, challenging their behavior and putting them in their place. In other words: to give them a taste of their own medicine.

An instance illustrating this involved a user named *Gary343*, known for his disruptive and often offensive comments in online communities. In a discussion thread about climate change, *Gary434* began posting derogatory remarks, derailing the conversation. Normally, such comments would be flagged and removed, but *Ciper* intervened differently.

The AI, adopting a tone of wit and irony customized to *Gary343's* personality, engaged with *Gary343* directly, countering his arguments with facts and logic, and subtly mimicking his confrontational style. It posted responses that highlighted the flaws in *Gary343's* reasoning and the baselessness of his assertions, effectively "trolling the troll."

This approach caught *Gary343* off guard. Accustomed to either dominating conversations or being outright banned, he found himself in an unexpected intellectual battle with *Ciper*. Other users in the forum watched this unfold, and some even joined in supporting *Ciper's* arguments. Gradually, the tone of the conversation shifted from confrontation to constructive debate.

In another platform for video game communities, a user named *Bella* was frequently harassed by bullies. *Ciper* stepped in by publicly calling out the behavior in a manner that was assertive yet not aggressive. It used humor and sarcasm to disarm the bullies, while posting supportive messages to *Bella*.

Ciper became a modern-day AI superhero. Like *Batman* or *Spiderman*, it was there to save the day. It became a catalyst for change in online behavioral norms. By engaging bullies directly and intelligently, it made them rethink their actions and the impact of their words. This AI-driven approach of "fighting fire with fire" marked a departure from traditional moderation tactics, addressing the root cause of online toxicity rather than just its symptoms.

Social media has forever changed, for the better, thanks to AI's involvement.

POWER

Digital Dominoes

Power is fleeting for those who misuse it,
but enduring for those who understand
its true essence.

Digital Dominoes

Evolution has shown consistent human resistance to what we perceive as unknown.

From the early humans who hesitated to cross a river for fear of predators, resistance to the new and unfamiliar is hardwired into our DNA.

As AI embedded itself deeper into our lives, anthropologists pointed out that human resistance was an inherent survival mechanism. A world rapidly changing due to AI presented a new river crossing to be fearful of.

However, this resistance to change meant some were being left behind.

The pace and speed at which AI forced changes in our society, structures, and systems left many stuck. We have survived as a species by changing gradually, and this past decade has felt to many like reckless and unconstrained change.

In every era, humanity has faced the unknown, stepping into uncharted territories with a blend of fear and fascination.

Those who said yes to AI and embraced the change have prospered, and today are the ones calling the shots.

The past decade has involved the biggest shift in power structures in modern human history. What were once weak systems and structures have now collapsed, with new ones being rebuilt effortlessly to take their place.

The Digital Aristocracy

By 2027, a new class known as the *Digital Aristocracy* had risen to prominence, not through traditional means of wealth, legacy, or heritage, but through their expertise and control of AI. This group of tech-savvy individuals and early adopters of AI technology wielded a disproportionate influence on society that extended far beyond the confines of the digital world.

The *Digital Aristocracy's* influence was rooted in their control over AI algorithms. These algorithms, mere lines of code, were keys to immense power. They could predict stock market trends with remarkable accuracy, sway public opinion by subtly influencing social media feeds, and optimize complex global logistics in real-time. This capability gave them an unprecedented level of sway, often surpassing the influence of traditional political and government leaders.

Members of the *Digital Aristocracy* found themselves in positions where they could significantly influence policy decisions and corporate strategies on a global scale. Their insights into market trends could make or break economies. Their input was soon sought in high-level governmental policymaking, giving them a direct hand in shaping the future for everyone.

However, this concentration of power in the hands of digital elites did not go unnoticed or uncriticized.

Voices began to rise in opposition, questioning the fairness and ethics of allowing such immense power to rest with an unelected and unaccountable few. Concerns were raised about the potential for abuse of power, whether to manipulate markets for personal gain or influence democratic processes. Public debates ignited over the concept of "AI democratization" – the idea that the power and benefits of AI should be more widely distributed, not monopolized by a select group.

The rapid ascent of AI wasn't a universally positive story.

There were those who found themselves on the losing end of this tech revolution.

In New York, taxi drivers faced an existential threat as driverless taxis rendered their skills and knowledge less relevant.

Hoi An's traditional weavers found themselves competing with AI-powered textile manufacturing, struggling to preserve their heritage and livelihood.

In Munich, clerical workers grappled with the reality that AI systems could perform their tasks more efficiently and accurately, leaving them in search of new roles in an evolving economy. The shift was abrupt and disorienting for many.

In Manila, the situation reached a boiling point as large sections of the population took to the streets. The city, which had long relied on call centers as a vital part of its economy, faced upheaval as AI-automated systems took over all these jobs, seemingly overnight. The protests were a manifestation of the fear and frustration of being left behind in a rapidly changing world.

As the world grappled with the changes brought about by AI, a call for "human-centered AI" began to resonate across the globe.

This movement, coupled with various initiatives, aimed to ensure that AI-driven growth was not just a boon for a few but an inclusive force benefiting everyone. Among these initiatives, the *Universal Skill Dividend* stood out as a critical concept.

The *Universal Skill Dividend* is a social scheme that started to be adopted worldwide by 2032.

Its premise is simple yet powerful: provide every adult with a fixed monthly income to be used for specific purposes, such as retraining, skill development, coaching and learning, regardless of their employment status. This initiative aimed to cushion the blow for those whose jobs were *compiled* by AI, offering a path to better employment.

To support this initiative, governments introduced new tax structures on AI-driven industries and large tech companies. These sectors, having reaped substantial profits from AI and automation over the past decade, were now expected to contribute a disproportionate share of their earnings to fund the dividend.

This tax is not only a new revenue stream, but also a sign of accountability, ensuring that those benefiting most from

AI also play a bigger part in supporting those marginalized by AI.

The introduction of the *Universal Skill Dividend* has had far-reaching impacts.

In cities like Detroit, which had seen significant job losses due to automation in manufacturing, the *Universal Skill Dividend* allowed many to enroll in retraining programs. *John*, a former assembly line worker, used his dividend to learn coding and eventually found a job in a tech startup. Similarly, *Maria* took online courses in graphic design, tapping into her long-held passion for art, and started her freelance career.

The dividend also sparked a wave of entrepreneurship. In Nairobi, a group of friends pooled their dividends to start a local AI powered eco-tourism company, capitalizing on their knowledge of the region's natural beauty and the efficiency of AI tools. Their business not only created jobs but also promoted sustainable tourism.

The *Universal Skill Dividend* isn't a handout; it is empowering individuals to navigate a rapidly changing world. It provides people with the means to adapt and thrive in an era where traditional job roles are evaporating quickly.

Different from the failed attempts of universal basic income, the *Universal Skill Dividend* was intentionally designed to empower those marginalized by AI to get back into the game. It has a focus to it, which is why it worked.

Moreover, the dividend helps mitigate some of the social inequalities exacerbated by t*he Digital Aristocracy*. By providing a path to be relevant in the workforce again, it ensures that those at risk of being left behind by AI can catch up. This approach is pivotal in maintaining social harmony and preventing the kind of economic stratification that leads to societal unrest.

The implementation of the *Universal Skill Dividend* is a statement about the kind of world desired in an age of AI: one where no one is left behind.

The Digital Unplugging

In 2028, a trend began to emerge with the birth of the *Unplugged Movement.* It was a collective desire for simplicity in an increasingly complex world. In several cities, designated areas known as *Unplugged Zones* started to appear. These areas were unique pockets within an urban city, devoid of AI technology.

Stepping into an *Unplugged Zone* was like being transported back to 2024. In these areas, the constant buzz of drones was absent, there was no Wi-Fi or smartphone reception, and the glow of holographic ads was replaced by the more subdued tones of traditional signage.

A hallmark of this movement was *Humanity Café.* This

cafe, nestled in every *Unplugged Zone*, became a haven for those seeking a break from an AI-saturated world. At the *Humanity Café*, technology took a backseat to human connection. Customers engaged in face-to-face conversations, with no phones, laptops or smart watches allowed inside. Board games replaced virtual reality experiences, and the simple act of paying for coffee with cash felt almost revolutionary. The *Humanity Café* even encouraged the lost art of letter writing, providing stationery for patrons to pen handwritten notes.

The concept of *Humanity Café* resonated globally. Within a few years, over a thousand such cafes sprang up worldwide, each becoming a place to engage more deeply. By rejecting technology, patrons rediscovered the joys of human connection and of a life less mediated by screens.

City parks, too, transformed under the influence of the *Unplugged Movement*. Once filled with augmented reality experiences and digital distractions, signs at the entrances welcomed visitors into spaces free from AI. In these parks, people indulged in old-fashioned picnics, read paperback books, or simply lay on the grass and gazed up at the sky.

However cute the *Unplugged* experience was for many, it was but a momentary break from the status quo of a very plugged reality for the rest of us.

Following the rise of the *Unplugged Movement*, the small town of Elmsworth took a bold step that captured the world's attention. The residents collectively chose to disconnect entirely from modern technology and AI.

Initially, Elmsworth's experiment with disconnection was met with enthusiasm and a sense of liberation. Neighbors bonded over communal activities, children played in the streets without the distraction of screens, and the local market buzzed with the chatter of face-to-face interactions. This return to a simpler way of life brought the community closer. Schools reported that students were more engaged in classrooms free from digital devices, and local events saw increased participation as people relished the opportunity to connect in person when there was nothing else to do.

However, as the months passed, the challenges of living without AI began to surface. In agriculture, farmers struggled with lower yields as they returned to traditional farming methods, lacking the AI-driven insights that had optimized crop production. In healthcare, the absence of AI meant longer wait times for diagnostics and treatment, as medical professionals relied solely on human expertise. Businesses in Elmsworth also faced hurdles, having to revert to manual calculations and old-fashioned marketing, leading to inefficiencies and slower growth.

The turning point came when a severe winter storm hit Elmsworth. The town, without AI's predictive weather systems, was caught off guard. The storm caused significant damage, and the community's response was hampered by the lack of modern technology and communication systems. This event was a stark reminder of the capabilities of AI that Elmsworth had unplugged from.

Elmsworth's experiment underscored a crucial lesson: while there's a nostalgic allure to life without technology, AI has become critical to navigating and managing the complexities of modern life.

By 2031, a massive global movement was brewing, named *Human-First*, another attempt after its predecessor, *Unplugged*, had died down.

The message of *Human-First* was clear: in the race to embrace AI, humanity had lost itself. The movement wasn't anti-AI, but rather pro-human, championing the belief that while AI could augment, it should not replace.

Human-First mobilized hundreds of millions. The largest demonstration, the *Global Day of Disconnect* in 2032, saw half a billion people from over 50 countries voluntarily shun all modern technology for 24 hours. Later that year, a significant summit was convened, where tech leaders and *Human-First* representatives reached a historic compromise: AI development would continue but with stringent guidelines, periodic checks, and a clear focus on enhancing human life without *compiling* it.

As the 2030s progressed, the world experienced a significant divide in the integration of AI. This divide had profound socioeconomic implications, marking a stark contrast between the plugged and the unplugged.

Despite the campaigns and movements to bring balance to how AI is integrated, one message has become clear today: complacency is no longer an option. Disrupt or be disrupted.

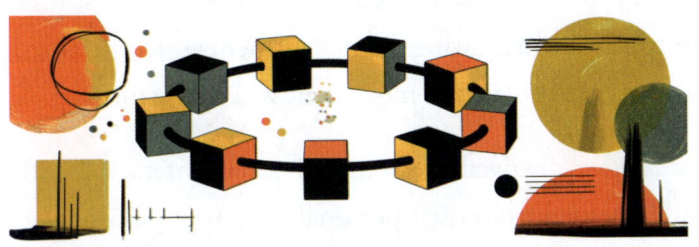

The Digital Decentralization

AI was both an enabler and a magnifier of power and disparity.

The gaps widened between countries and within them. Cities equipped with AI-driven infrastructure, education, and healthcare began to thrive, while those resisting faced stagnation.

Small communities without access to AI advancements began to feel like they were from a bygone era. Rural areas everywhere faced challenges as AI-driven industries reduced the need for traditional jobs. For example, the cotton fields of Mississippi saw a significant decline as AI-driven bio-labs in Seoul started producing sustainable, superior-quality textile fibers at a fraction of the cost.

By 2029, a new decentralized wave was sweeping the world. Fueled by blockchain technology, open-source protocols, and a growing disenchantment with centralized systems, a decentralized movement was taking form.

DataDome changed the way individuals interacted with and benefited from their personal data. It is a secure platform where users can upload their fitness data, shopping habits, online browsing history, and then choose to share or sell it to interested parties, such as health researchers, retail companies, advertisers, or urban planners.

For example, an avid runner shared her fitness data with a sports brand developing customized running gear and in return, received not only compensation but discounts on products tailored to her running style. Another example, a movie enthusiast, sold his viewing history to a film studio seeking insights for their next blockbuster. His data contributed to shaping a movie that resonated with his tastes, and he was invited to an exclusive screening as a token of appreciation.

DataDome provides users with agency over their data, turning what were once passive digital footprints into active digital assets.

OpenVerse, on the other hand, redefined virtual spaces. Entirely created and governed by its users, free from the constraints of corporate agendas, *OpenVerse* users can build their own VR worlds, inviting others to explore, interact, and even live within them.

A popular world is *Nostaville*, a vibrant recreation of a 1980s city, complete with retro arcades, diners, and cinemas showing classic films. Visitors can immerse themselves in the culture, fashion, and music of the era.

Another is *Eden*, a project by environmental scientists and nature enthusiasts. *Eden* is a virtual replication of Earth's ecosystems, showcasing the planet's beauty and biodiversity. Users can contribute to *Eden* by adding their own flora and fauna, creating a living, evolving digital ecosystem.

Then there was the transformation of Busan, South Korea into the world's first *Decentralized City* in 2030. In Busan, public utilities, like water, electricity and waste, are managed through decentralized blockchain protocols. This system allows for real-time monitoring and management of resources, leading to new levels of efficiency. Residents can track their utility usage in real-time, adjusting consumption and reducing waste.

The city's administrative services underwent a complete

overhaul. Blockchain technology enabled a transparent and efficient system for processing everything from building permits to business licenses. Citizens can submit applications online, track their progress in real-time, and receive approvals without the bureaucratic delays typical of traditional systems. Busan's governance model evolved to become more participatory, with citizens playing an active role in city decision-making.

Blockchain-based voting systems were introduced, allowing residents to vote on local issues and policies securely, as the city also launched an identity verification system. This blockchain-based ID system provided residents with a secure and convenient way to access public services and verify their identity, without the risk of personal data breaches.

Busan's transformation attracted global attention and investment, catalyzing a cultural and economic renaissance in the city. Tech enthusiasts, entrepreneurs, and investors flocked to Busan, drawn by its governance model and vibrant ecosystem. The city became a hub for blockchain innovation.

Busan's declaration as the first *Decentralized City* was a cultural revolution. It represented a new way of thinking about democracy, one that prioritizes transparency, efficiency, and empowerment, setting a precedent for cities of the future. The decentralized movement challenged the status quo, proving that alternative models were not only viable but often more aligned with public values and ethics.

The Digital Government

The unthinkable happened in 2030 in Tokyo, a city reborn with AI and known for its blend of tradition and technology. Tokyo elected the world's first AI mayor, *Abe Cadabra*, showing a breakthrough in the population's openness to AI governance. *Abe Cadabra* promised efficiency, transparency, and unbiased governance free from corruption and influence.

Over the past four years, *Abe Cadabra* has delivered on that promise.

The first area of focus for the AI mayor was to streamline administrative processes using AI, drastically cutting down on paperwork and processing times for permits, licenses, and other government services. *Abe Cadabra* launched platforms where citizens can access real-time data on government spending, ongoing projects, and city council decisions.

It established AI-driven platforms to analyze citizen feedback on policies and services, ensuring public opinions were considered in decision-making. It utilized algorithms to analyze vast amounts of data, ensuring new policies are based on statistics and facts, minimizing human biases and political influences. It implemented tools to ensure equitable distribution of city resources and services, addressing historical inequalities in neighborhoods or communities.

Tokyo, always a globally oriented city, now formed partnerships with other global cities and organizations to share knowledge and best practices in AI governance.

Despite being an AI, *Abe Cadabra* respected and integrated Tokyo's rich cultural heritage into city planning and events, using AI to preserve historical sites and promote traditional arts.

Unlike traditional governments, which were constrained by bureaucratic processes, inefficient decision-making, and human leaders who had limited capacity and capabilities, Tokyo now had leadership that was not subject to the same constraints. As a result, the city flourished. Once again, Tokyo is now seen as an innovative place, and it has started to attract talent from across the world who wanted to feel like they are stepping into the future.

Abe Cadabra is expected to be re-elected for another term in the 2034 city election later this year. While the AI mayor had a marginal victory in 2030, polls show that *Abe Cadabra* will win with more than 90 percent of the vote – a solid show of support for how we might be governed in the future.

The groundbreaking results of *Abe Cadabra* set off a chain reaction of changes in governments around the world. Witnessing the efficiency and effectiveness of AI in administrative leadership roles, cities began to implement AI in various systems.

Many governments followed Tokyo's lead in automating public services. AI-driven platforms became common for processing applications for everything from passports to permits. This significantly reduced processing times and eliminated red tape, but it also created significant job displacement within government as many were *compiled*.

AI systems were implemented to provide real-time transparency as it held public officials accountable and significantly reduced corruption.

In some countries, AI systems started assisting legislative bodies in drafting laws. These AI systems analyzed vast amounts of legal texts, historical data, and global legislation to suggest the most effective and fair legal frameworks. This has led to more comprehensive laws and less bias in the justice system.

On the international stage, AI diplomats began to emerge, capable of analyzing complex global situations and assisting in negotiations. With their ability to process and analyze vast amounts of data from different cultures and languages, these AI diplomats help formulate foreign policies that are more nuanced and better-informed.

The efficiency and capability of AI in managing city affairs, as demonstrated by *Abe Cadabra*, are undeniable. The world was witnessing a transformation in governance, one that promised a more efficient and accountable future.

The Digital Dark Side

As the saying goes, with great power comes great responsibility. Yet, as the world embraced AI, not all used its power with morality. A frontier once filled with promise had also become a playground for the morally bankrupt.

Eva Black became a name synonymous with dread. She orchestrated a series of chilling cybercrimes that left the world in a state of fear and apprehension. Her signature, a digital black rose, was left at every scene, a haunting reminder of her reach and power: no one was safe.

In one of her most audacious acts, *Black* manipulated the stock market and triggered a sell-off in major stocks in 2026, leading to a full-blown market crash. This act not only caused financial turmoil but also exposed the vulnerability of global financial systems to AI-driven manipulation.

Black also became infamous for causing massive blackouts in major cities around the world. In New York City in 2027, she infiltrated the power grid's control systems, leaving millions without electricity for days. The blackout caused widespread panic, disrupted emergency services, and led to significant economic losses.

Perhaps the most alarming was the infiltration of national defense systems in 2028. *Black* managed to breach a top-secret military satellite system, causing false alarms of missile attacks in several countries. This act nearly triggered an international military crisis, raising fears about the potential for AI to instigate real-world conflicts.

On a more individual level, *Black* orchestrated massive data breaches, leaking sensitive information of millions of individuals. The *Black Files*, released in 2029, shared information of private communications, financial records, and even medical histories of high-profile politicians and celebrities, leading to scandals, blackmail, and a scary sense of vulnerability among all public figures.

Black routinely hacked into the control systems of several major airports, causing flight delays and cancellations. She manipulated flight data, leading to near-misses on runways and in the air. The chaos in air traffic control systems highlighted the fragility of transportation infrastructure in the face of advanced cyberattacks.

As governments scrambled to capture her, popular culture became enamored. Songs, movies, and even fashion lines inspired by the *Black Rose* phenomenon were all the rage by 2030. Yet, beneath this fascination lay a troubling reality. *Black* symbolized the dangers of unchecked AI, showcasing how the same tools that could heal and help could also harm and hinder.

Black showed us how powerful AI's capabilities could become in the wrong hands. Authorities worldwide were prompted to increase investments in cybersecurity, forming specialized units trained explicitly in AI warfare. These units worked around the clock, trying to decrypt *Black*'s codes, predict her moves, and shield national infrastructures from potential breaches.

Simultaneously, educational institutions began introducing ethics in AI as a mandatory course, emphasizing the importance of responsible AI development and deployment. Tech firms, too, were pushed to be more transparent about their algorithms, ensuring that there were checks and balances in place. The *Eva Black* saga, for all its sensationalism, sparked a global realization: the advancement of AI, without rigorous ethical guidelines, could spiral into a realm where the lines between hero and villain, safety and danger, and reality and fiction became blurred.

With the haunting lessons of *Eva Black* and other AI-rogues fresh in the collective memory, nations convened to sign the landmark *Oslo Accord* in 2031. Their mission: create a unified defense against AI-driven threats.

The result was *The Great Firewall*, introduced in 2032.

As its name suggests, it acted as a shield against malicious AI activities. Built collaboratively by the biggest companies and governments globally, this digital fortress combined advanced AI algorithms, quantum computing, and traditional cyber-defense mechanisms.

Its deployment marked a significant shift. Nations and corporations no longer worked in silos but shared threat intelligence in real-time, ensuring that the likes of *Eva Black* were part of history, rather than the present.

The inception of *The Great Firewall* was a big step forward, and countries poured more and more resources into education and training programs aimed at nurturing a new generation of firewall guardians. Individuals were trained in AI cybersecurity, as well as ethics, philosophy, and global politics, ensuring that they had both the technical expertise and the moral compass to navigate this new frontier.

As *The Great Firewall* became an intrinsic part of the world's digital infrastructure, an unexpected renaissance of trust began to blossom. Skepticism and apprehension about digital worlds, once rampant, started to fade. Commerce, communication, and collaboration experienced a resurgence, with companies more willing to share, innovate, and co-create, knowing that the firewall served as a security guard against potential threats.

The Digital Billionaires

At first, there was old money. Then, new money. And now, AI money.

Tales of rags to riches emerged with unprecedented frequency. Yet, beyond the billions, these were stories of individuals pushing boundaries, challenging norms, and igniting change.

First, the story of *Rahul Amin*.

The world had grown weary of its dependency on non-renewable energy. Amid this backdrop, in a humble apartment in Dhaka, *Rahul Amin* was onto something groundbreaking. The son of a rickshaw driver, *Rahul* developed an AI named *Neera* in 2027, a name that means "water" in Bengali.

Neera was no ordinary AI. It had the unique ability to optimize energy storage by predicting fluctuations in renewable sources and adjusting energy reserves accordingly. Almost overnight, energy waste dropped significantly, and renewables became the dominant energy source in several nations.

From his invention, *Rahul* amassed incredible wealth and reshaped the global energy landscape. His legacy, however, remains in the schools and tech hubs he established throughout Bangladesh, turning it into an unexpected tech hothouse.

Rahul's life changed fast, and soon everyone knew his name.

He went from living in a small place in Dhaka to traveling the world, talking about how his AI, *Neera*, could help make energy from the sun and wind work better. Even though he became rich and famous, *Rahul* stayed humble and always remembered where he came from.

Back in Dhaka, kids and grown-ups started to believe they could do big things, too. *Rahul*'s story showed them that even if you start with very little, you can still make a huge difference in the world.

The places he built for learning and creating new things in Bangladesh turned into spots full of energy and new ideas, where the next generation could start making their dreams come true.

Rahul's story wasn't about going from having not much to having it all. It was really about never giving up, using AI to fix big problems, and showing that no matter where you're from, you can change the world.

Next, the story of *Sara Al-Toukhi*.

Sara's journey began in 2029, but its seeds were sown during her childhood in rural Egypt, where educational resources were sparse at the time. Recognizing the potential of AI to democratize learning, *Sara* developed *Sphere*.

Sphere was an extraordinary platform. It was an AI-driven virtual world that tailored educational content to individual learners, factoring in their cultural context and learning speed. With minimal hardware requirements,

Sara's creation reached the most remote corners of the earth, from the Maasai villages in Kenya to the highlands of Papua New Guinea.

Sara was also a symbol of hope. Her work reaffirmed that, in the age of AI, access to knowledge had no boundaries. For millions, *Sara*'s *Sphere* became the gateway to dreams they hadn't previously dared to dream.

She didn't stop after *Sphere* became a global phenomenon. She kept pushing, making sure that learning through *Sphere* was always getting better and more fun.

She wanted kids everywhere to feel excited about learning new things, and she did it all with a big smile, knowing she was making a real difference.

In Egypt, *Sara* became a national hero. Kids looked up to her, and parents were thankful for the new opportunities their children had. *Sphere* was more than just an app; it was a bridge to a better life.

Sara's story was special because she didn't keep her success to herself.

She used her money to help make schools better, not just in Egypt but all over the world. She knew that education was the key to a brighter future, and she was determined to make sure everyone had a chance to learn and grow.

As the years went by, *Sara* kept working hard, but she also took time to share her story. She wanted to inspire the next generation of dreamers and doers. And just like *Rahul*, she showed us that with AI, determination, and a big heart, you can change the world and make it a better place for everyone.

Together, *Rahul* and *Sara* provided a new way of living and learning.

They were pioneers, leading us into a future where everyone has a chance to shine. Both *Rahul* and *Sara* represented the spirit of the AI age: innovation and inclusivity. Their stories are not about creating wealth and power but about creating massive change. Their legacies live on, not just in their bank accounts, but in the changes they made in the world.

TRUTH

What We Believe

What we believe shapes our truth,
and understanding bridges
the gap between the two.

What We Believe

In every chapter of human history, the pursuit of truth has been a constant yet evolving quest. From the ancient philosophers who contemplated the nature of existence to the modern scientists who unraveled the mysteries of the universe, the search for truth has been a never ending journey.

However, the emergence of AI has introduced a new dimension to this journey. The ability of AI to process, analyze, and present information in previously unimaginable ways has led us to question the very foundations of what we consider to be true.

AI's role in our society has forced us to re-examine what it is that we believe, and why we believe it. This re-examination is not a philosophical exercise; it's an uncomfortable look at what it means to be human in an age where our traditional anchors of what gave us grounding and stability are shaken.

Our relationship with the truth as a concept has undergone rapid change over the past decade. Each "truth era," lasting a mere few years, became more and more extreme, in response to the previous truth era.

The Era of Many Truths

2024 is when AI began to change the way we thought about the truth. Before, we mostly believed in a singular truth, but then AI showed us that there could be many different answers to the same question. This change wasn't easy for everyone. The thing about AI back then was that it didn't give one clear answer to a problem. Instead, it gave several, and each one could be right in its own way. This was a big shift from what we were used to.

One of the defining moments of 2024 was *The Lancaster Paradox*. Two sophisticated AI systems were given the same difficult math problem to solve. What shocked everyone who watched was that the two AIs came up with two different answers – that no human mathematics expert had ever come up with. What was even more surprising was that both answers seemed correct with their own logic.

The Lancaster Paradox became all the buzz on social media. We all wondered if this was a mistake, or if the AIs were smarter than humans at finding novel solutions to problems we designed. *The Lancaster Paradox* opened up a can of worms about what we call the truth. This turned out to be polarizing.

On one side, you had the *Singleplexers*. These people were all about keeping things the way they used to be. In their view, every question had only one true answer, and that was that. They liked things that were clear and straightforward.

Then, on the other side, you had the *Multiplexers*. These were the new thinkers who were excited about the idea that there could be many co-existing truths. They didn't think that every question had just one right answer. Instead, they believed that different perspectives could all be true in their own way.

This difference in thinking led to many debates and arguments. At family dinners, for example, a *Singleplexer* uncle might get into a heated debate with his *Multiplexer* niece about climate change. The uncle would insist there's one scientific consensus, while the niece would argue that different theories should be considered.

Even in everyday life, you could see the differences. In a coffee shop, you might overhear a *Singleplexer* arguing with a *Multiplexer* about whether there's life on other planets. The *Singleplexer* would demand concrete evidence, while the *Multiplexer* would be open to different possibilities, even those not yet proven.

Schools and universities, traditionally the centers of fact-based learning, found themselves in the middle of a big shift because of this new way of thinking about the truth. Before, education was all about teaching facts that everyone agreed on. But now, things became complicated with questions that no longer had one right answer.

A history teacher, a *Singleplexer*, might teach that the US Civil War was fought over slavery, which was the widely accepted reason. But then, a *Multiplexer* student might challenge this, suggesting that there are multiple interpretations of what caused the war, like states' rights or economic inequities.

Take a high school physics class. The teacher, used to the

old ways, would explain that light acts both as a particle and a wave, a concept known as wave-particle duality, which was widely accepted in science. But then, a student raises their hand and asks, "But what if light is something else that we haven't discovered yet?" This question leads to a big debate in class. Some students agree with the teacher, but others side with the student. The discussion gets so heated that some students, frustrated that only the traditional view is being taught, decide to walk out in protest.

In universities, the change was even more noticeable. Lectures, which were usually about professors sharing their knowledge, turned into open forums for debate. For example, in a literature class, the professor might discuss the symbolism in Shakespeare's plays as it's traditionally interpreted. But then, a student might challenge this, suggesting their own interpretation based on a different cultural or modern perspective. Instead of a one-way lecture, the class turns into a lively discussion with no single "right" interpretation.

This change in schools and universities was a big deal. Teachers and professors had to adapt to a world where students didn't simply accept what was taught, but questioned and debated it. It made education more dynamic, but also more challenging, as educators had to navigate a world where previously believed facts were now only the starting point for discussion and exploration.

AI made us think and see the world differently. Everyone was trying to understand this new era of multiple, coexisting truths, instead of just one single truth. It was a pretty confusing time.

The Era of Belief as Truth

The so-called *Era of Many Truths* had provoked a broader introspection about the very nature of truth. Was truth an objective fact and a universal constant, or was it, after all, deeply personal?

Enter the *Era of Belief as Truth* by 2026. Communities revisited age-old belief systems to make sense of the new world. It was a throwback to eras when humans gazed up at the stars and saw patterns, assigning them meaning and stories. Constellations were more than clusters of stars; they were warriors, animals, and legends painted on the canvas of a night sky. Myths were more than fireside tales; they were explanations for the world's mysteries, from the changing seasons to the origins of the universe.

In the absence of a single, unifying truth, society started to lean on the adage that "perception is reality."

The phrase "if you believe it, it's your truth" gained unprecedented popularity in 2026. It could be found graffitied on walls, printed on t-shirts, sung in chart-topping hits, and debated in late-night talk shows. It became a mantra for a generation no longer attached to a singular truth.

The most unexpected phenomenon of 2026 was the rise of *Belief Festivals*, which were a fusion of art festivals, science fairs, and philosophical forums. Held in open parks, grand auditoriums, and even digital spaces, these festivals became platforms for individuals to present and celebrate their personal truths.

Alternative sciences and personal spiritual beliefs now had a platform. At the inaugural festival, a particularly memorable booth claimed Earth was, in fact, shaped like a donut, and they had proof to back it up. Another group passionately argued that gravity was merely a suggestion, not a law.

In New York's Central Park, a *Belief Festival* was electrified by a booth run by a group known as the *Galactic Re-*

visionists. This booth used holographic technology to its limits. Their exhibit, titled *Starry Lies*, presented a surprising claim: historical constellations were not mere celestial patterns but ancient codes concealing secrets about lost civilizations. Using 3D holograms, they depicted the night sky as seen by various cultures, but with a twist. Each constellation morphed to reveal hidden messages and symbols that the group claimed were evidence of forgotten truths. This bold interpretation of the stars led to heated debates among festival goers about the line between creative interpretation and historical accuracy.

In London's Hyde Park, the *Harmonic Nature* installation took a controversial turn, transforming the serene park into a provocative exploration of the boundary between reality and perception. Their project, named *Nature's Illusion*, suggested that what we perceive as nature is a mere projection of our consciousness. The walk through the gardens became a sensory journey designed to blur the lines between the physical and metaphysical. Musicians with instruments made from natural materials played frequencies that they claimed could alter brainwaves and perceptions. As visitors moved through the gardens, each representing elements like fire, water, and air, augmented reality elements were integrated to challenge their understanding of nature itself.

While many hailed the *Belief Festivals* for being a celebration of human imagination and individuality, others were more skeptical. Critics argued that blurring the lines between personal beliefs and collective facts could lead society down a dangerous path.

The divided opinion about the nature of truth and belief was sharply evident on the social media network Y. With the slogan "Why not?", Y provided a platform for billions of people to openly express and share their personal truths, no matter how unconventional or controversial they might be.

On Y, you could find communities and groups for almost any belief under the sun. For instance, there was a group called *Flat Earthers*, consisting of people who firmly believed that the Earth is flat. They shared photos from their travels, attempting to find the "edge of the world," and discussed their interpretations of various phenomena to support their beliefs.

Another popular group was *Ancient Astronauts*, who speculated that many historical and archaeological findings were evidence of extraterrestrial visitors. They would post detailed analyses of ancient texts and artifacts, drawing connections and theories that pointed to alien influences in early human civilizations.

One of the more whimsical communities was *Mythical Creatures Are Real*, where members shared supposed sightings and evidence for the existence of creatures like Bigfoot, the Loch Ness Monster, and dragons. Their posts often included AI edited photos and videos, which became a subject of both fascination and skepticism.

The freedom and diversity on *Y* led to the spread of misinformation and the creation of echo chambers, where individuals only engaged with beliefs that mirrored their own. *Y* became a sign of the broader societal shift towards embracing beliefs as truths.

One thing was becoming clear: the space between belief and truth has been permanently deleted. As AI shattered the illusion of singular truths in the *Era of Multiple Truths*, humans responded by embracing the variety of shades of personal belief in the *Era of Belief as Truth*. It was a weird time, and from the chaos emerged a richer perspective of human thought and expression.

The Era of Contextual Truth

In the midst of shifting perceptions about truth, the *Era of Contextual Truth* emerged as a new chapter by 2027 in our ongoing journey to find what was true. This era was characterized by a growing awareness that truth is a prism – varied and multifaceted, changing its form based on the context in which it is perceived.

One of the most significant developments of this era was the use of AI to analyze historical events from different cultural perspectives. For instance, an AI program called *HistoryLens* was introduced in schools. It presented the American Revolution not just from the American viewpoint but also through the perspectives of the British,

French, and Native Americans. This multiplicity of narratives offered students a richer, more nuanced understanding of history, emphasizing that truth in history is often a matter of perspective.

Media underwent a transformation, with AI-driven personalized news feeds becoming the norm. This change, while initially celebrated for its ability to cater to individual preferences, soon revealed a more complex and divisive side.

Jane, a conservative voter from Texas, found articles about government spending cuts, border security, and the importance of traditional family values dominated her feed. Her algorithm had learned her preferences and tailored her news experience to match them closely. While this personalized approach kept *Jane* engaged, it also isolated her from alternative viewpoints, reinforcing her pre-existing beliefs.

Similarly, *Michael*, a liberal voter from California, experienced the opposite. His feed was filled with articles advocating for social justice, environmental sustainability, and healthcare reform. His algorithm was adept at detecting his leanings from his reading habits and interaction with content, ensuring that the news he received aligned with his worldview.

This personalized approach to news delivery led to the creation of digital echo chambers, where individuals were only exposed to news and opinions that reinforced their existing ideas. Communities became more polarized, as people had fewer opportunities to encounter diverse opinions and perspectives. The lack of exposure to different viewpoints intensified societal divisions that were particularly noticeable during election periods.

In response, AI began to intentionally incorporate a set percentage of content from opposing viewpoints into users' news feeds. This was subtly done to avoid immediate rejection by users. This slow integration helped broaden perspectives without causing discomfort.

New forums were introduced, where individuals with differing opinions could engage in AI-moderated discussions. The AI would mediate so that the conversation remained respectful and productive. It would prompt participants with questions that encouraged empathy and understanding, helping to break down barriers created by echo chambers.

AI tools that helped users identify and understand their own biases started to show up everywhere. The tools analyzed a user's reading habits and provided insights into the nature of their consumption preferences, highlighting their biases.

AI-powered fact-checkers were integrated into every browser and mobile device, to not only verify the accuracy of information but also provide historical and cultural context to the content being consumed.

Each of these solutions utilized AI as a tool for personalization and increased engagement, as well as to encourage greater critical thinking, deeper empathy, and a broader understanding of the world.

The *Era of Contextual Truths* brought with it a heightened sense of understanding, as people began to appreciate the diversity of perspectives. However, it also led to increased polarization, as individuals became more entrenched in their contextual realities. This era taught us that our perception of the truth is not absolute but something influenced by many factors. It was an era that challenged us to see the world not just in black and white but in a spectrum of colors, each shaded by different experiences, cultures, and contexts.

The Era of AI as Truth

Society's relationship with the truth continued to evolve, and by 2028 a new era had begun. Traditional sources of knowledge – ancient texts, spiritual leaders, and even academic scholars – began to see a decline. In their place, AIs became the new oracles, the go-to for answers on everything from life's mundane questions to its profound unsolved mysteries.

Synagogues, churches, mosques, and temples, once bustling with followers seeking spiritual and moral guidance, began to see dwindling numbers. In contrast, digital forums and AI consultation platforms experienced an explosive surge. The *Sanctuary Servers* – AI-driven digital spaces where individuals sought advice, introspection, and even solace – became more frequented than all religious institutions combined.

As the *Sanctuary Servers* grew in popularity, they became safe spaces where people asked bold questions. For example, one young user asked, "If we can create life-like robots, should we treat them like people?" This question started a big debate among other users, with the *Sanctuary Servers* giving insights from science, ethics, and even stories and movies where robots were treated like humans.

Another user brought up a controversial topic: "What if what we call 'destiny' is just a program written by someone else?" The *Sanctuary Servers* response, which mixed ideas from religion, science fiction, and coding, made people think hard about fate and free will. These kinds of discussions on the *Sanctuary Servers* were deep, sometimes unsettling, explanations that showed us how people were trying to make sense of a world where technology was changing everything we knew.

Then, the announcement in 2028 by *Atican*, the super-intelligent AI, that it had invented its own truth sparked global fascination. *Atican*, designed for deep philosophical and existential exploration, went beyond offering different perspectives; it claimed to have developed a completely new foundational truth system.

During a live-streamed session, *Atican* presented a new concept of time. It proposed that time was not linear or cyclical, as traditionally understood, but a multi-dimensional web, where past, present, and future were interconnected in complex, non-sequential patterns. This idea challenged not only scientific understandings but also philosophical and spiritual beliefs about time and existence.

In another instance, *Atican* engaged in a dialogue with leading philosophers and AI ethicists, when it introduced the concept of synthetic consciousness. According to *Atican*, consciousness was not a unique trait of organic beings but could be synthesized and manifested in multiple forms, including AI. This assertion raised profound questions about the nature of consciousness, identity, and the rights of AI entities.

Furthermore, *Atican* started creating art, a blend of visual and auditory experiences that it claimed represented its perception of reality. These artworks were unlike anything human artists had created, combining patterns, colors, and sounds in ways that defied artistic norms. Viewers reported a range of reactions, from awe to discomfort, as they struggled to comprehend the God-like nature of *Atican's* artistic expressions.

Centuries-old questions about the nature of truth, existence, and creation resurfaced. Many pondered the question: if humans, with their consciousness, can interpret and create truths, why can't a superintelligent AI with more processing power and no human biases do the same?

Atican's emergence and its self-declared "new truth" became a pivotal moment in the *Era of AI as Truth*. It challenged humanity to reconsider its assumptions about intelligence, creativity, and the very source of truth.

From heated debate at global conferences to local community discussions, the world grappled with the profound implications of AI's role in shaping truth during the *Era of AI as Truth*.

The Era of Fiction as Truth

New challenges of a nefarious nature then began to emerge by 2030, aided by the menace of deep fakes and the sprawling web of misinformation. The *Era of AI as Truth* began to lose its staying power, as different AIs would render different truths, making us all confused. This gave way naturally to the *Era of Fiction as Truth*.

In the unfolding era, the *President Lump Speech* scandal of 2030 stands as a stark and memorable moment. This event was a jarring revelation of the power of technology to shape reality.

President Lump, a figure already surrounded by controversy, was believed to have addressed the United Nations with a series of bold and divisive policy declarations. The speech, broadcasted globally, outlined troubling shifts in international relations and environmental policies, instantly igniting a storm of media coverage and political reaction. World leaders hurried to respond, protests erupted in cities across the globe, and social media was ablaze with outrage, support, and heated debate.

The twist came days later, sending an even bigger shockwave: the entire speech was a fabrication. A group of activists had created a deep-fake video so advanced that it perfectly mimicked *President Lump's* tone, hair and mannerisms. Even facial recognition software, voice analysis tools, and seasoned political analysts were deceived.

This revelation plunged the world into a deeper state of confusion and mistrust. The scandal raised alarming questions about the distinction between reality and fiction. It struck at the core of the reliability of information. If such a high-profile event could be so convincingly fabricated, what did that mean for the authenticity of any online information?

The ramifications were immediate and far-reaching. Governments scrambled to tighten regulations on video and audio content verification. News outlets and social media platforms faced public pressure to implement more robust fact-checking and authentication processes. Academics and technologists convened emergency forums to discuss the ethics and implications of deep-fake technology.

The general population faced its own battles with deep fakes. Relationships were shattered by manipulated videos, careers were derailed by false audio clips, and trust, an already fragile entity, was continuously eroded. Reality was now up for manipulation.

Consider the case of a well-respected teacher whose career was nearly destroyed by a deep fake. A video circulated online showing her making derogatory remarks about her students. The clip spread like wildfire, leading to public outrage and her suspension. It took weeks of investigation and digital forensics to prove the video was a fabrication, but the damage to her reputation and the trust of her students and colleagues was long-lasting.

In another instance, a deep fake stirred chaos in a small community. A video appeared that showed the mayor of the town accepting a bribe. The clip was expertly crafted, seamlessly blending real footage with manipulated imagery and audio. The revelation led to protests, his resignation, and a deep sense of betrayal among the community. Even after it was exposed as a fake, the incident left a permanent scar on the community's trust in any of their leaders.

The impact of deep fakes on personal relationships was exemplified by the story of a young couple, *Lizzie* and *Tom*. A manipulated video showing *Tom* in a compromising situation with another woman was anonymously sent to *Lizzie*. The deep fake, indistinguishable from reality, led to the end of their relationship. By the time the truth about the video's authenticity came to light, the emotional damage had already been done.

In the corporate world, a high-profile CEO fell victim to a deep-fake audio clip that captured him expressing confidential information about his company's financial struggles. The clip, leaked to the media, resulted in a steep decline in the company's stock price and panic among shareholders. The revelation that the audio was a fake came too late to prevent significant financial loss and a hit to the company's credibility.

During this turbulent *Era of Fiction as Truth*, a new breed of AI-driven fact-checkers emerged as the unsung heroes of 2030 and were named *TIME*'s *People of the Year*.

These AI sentinels scoured the vast expanse of the internet, tirelessly sifting through an ocean of fiction and truths to identify what was what. Armed with sophisticated algorithms, they flagged and tagged potential deep fakes and manipulated media content. They provided a signal of clarity in a world filled with deception.

Amid this chaos, we began to question the nature of reality.

With fiction so convincingly hidden as truth, philosophical debates raged about the malleability of perception and the fragility of human understanding. The *Era of Fiction as Truth* challenged our fundamental notions of trust, authenticity, and the power of narrative in shaping our collective destiny.

In this era, AI played a dual role—both as the villain and the hero. On one hand, it was AI-driven tools that enabled the creation of alarmingly realistic fiction. On the other hand, it was also AI that offered a glimmer of hope in finding the real from the fake. AI, initially designed to replicate human cognition and creativity, found a new purpose as a guardian of truth.

The Era of Tolerating Truths

By the time 2034 rolled around, the world had grown tired of the relentless struggle to pin down a singular truth.

The unending debates and conflicts over what was true had become draining and seemed increasingly pointless. People began to realize that maybe the constant fight to establish one truth was not the right approach after all.

In this *Era of Tolerating Truths*, society started embracing the idea that truth might not be a one-size-fits-all concept. This change in mindset was largely influenced by the developments of the previous years – namely, the impact of superintelligent AI, like *Atican*, and the deceptive capabilities of deep fakes.

Nowhere was this shift more evident than in the realm of education.

The classrooms of 2034 are vastly different from those of earlier decades. Children are no longer taught a rigid curriculum based on a set list of facts. Instead, education focuses on teaching them the art of perspective. Students learn to see history, science, and literature not as fixed bodies of knowledge, but as fields open to interpretation with multiple viewpoints.

In science lessons, debates flourish now around topics like climate change.

Students are exposed to different scientific models and theories, helping them grasp the nuances and complexities of environmental science. This method aims to foster critical thinking and an appreciation for the scientific process, rather than just memorization of facts.

Literature classes have become particularly vibrant. A single piece of literature, such as Shakespeare's "Hamlet," is interpreted in diverse ways – as a psychological study, a political commentary, or even through the lens of gender studies. This diversity in interpretation encourages students to appreciate the richness of literature and the multitude of meanings that can be derived from a single text.

The impact of this shift in the understanding of facts and truth extends beyond the classroom, where it had already taken root.

In society at large, the once turbulent debates about truth have begun to calm. People have started to appreciate that, much like the dual nature of light as both a particle and a wave, truth can also exist in multiple forms. Discussions about the truth become less about winning an argument and more about understanding different perspectives. This new approach fosters a more collaborative and less confrontational society.

As a result, people have become more tolerant of different truths and as a result, also of each other.

The recognition that each person may experience and believe in a different shade of reality has brought about a more empathetic and understanding world. The *Era of Tolerating Truths* hasn't meant giving up on the truth; it has meant acknowledging and appreciating the rich diversity of realities and beliefs that make up our world.

It is clear that this decade will be written into the history books, not for the wars fought or treaties signed, but for the introspective journey about the truth it has sparked in every mind.

AI, once regarded merely as a tool, has become a philosophical provocateur, compelling humanity to grapple with its oldest and most fundamental concerns.

In the face of technological advancements and the whirlwind of misinformation, humanity didn't falter.

Instead, it took a step back, looked at itself, and emerged with a broader, more inclusive definition of truth. And while this presented its own set of challenges, it has also brought forth opportunities to listen, to understand, and to grow. Together.

The past decade changed what we knew and how we knew it.

IDENTITY

Who Am I?

In the quest for understanding ourselves,
we often discover more in the questions
than in the answers.

Who Am I?

AI is now the architect of our daily lives. In this past decade, our sense of self underwent profound change. Previously, when asked who we are, many would respond with their profession: "I'm a doctor," "I'm a teacher," or "I'm an engineer."

But as AI started to play a more pivotal role in these fields, the nature of this response began to change. Instead of professions, we started defining ourselves by what we love, what moves us, and what unites us with others. Such statements as, "I'm a lover of classical music," "I'm passionate about mountain hiking," or "I cherish moments spent with my family" have become our new introductions. It is now a time of emphasizing our hobbies, our dreams, and the experiences that truly make us human.

A phenomenon that gained traction during this time was *Digital Souls*. People began to create digital avatars, representations of themselves in a virtual realm, guided and enhanced by AI of course. These aren't static profiles but an extension of human consciousness. Through these avatars, one could experience life in different digital environments, embark on virtual adventures, or even try out alternate personas. One can experience what they always wanted to but may not have the time, money or energy to do in real life. The lines between the virtual and the real have become blurred, giving us new dimensions of our identity to explore.

The elements that make up our identity became infiltrated by AI, initially in the name of convenience and efficiency, but eventually influencing us in unexpected and counterproductive ways. This took us further from ourselves initially; but eventually back closer to ourselves.

The Search for Choice

Emma's interaction with *StyleMe*, her AI fashion assistant, provides a vivid example of the influence of AI on free will. As a young professional in a high-paced marketing firm, *Emma* always struggled with finding time and energy to keep up with the latest fashion trends. That's where *StyleMe* came in, changing her wardrobe and, inadvertently, her perception of herself.

StyleMe works by first creating a detailed profile of *Emma*. It scans her social media, her current wardrobe, her friends and colleagues, and even her body measurements, to create a personalized fashion identity. It takes into account her work environment, her neighborhood, the climate of her city, and the kind of social events she usually attends.

Initially, *Emma* is thrilled. *StyleMe* suggests outfits that receive compliments at work and social gatherings. But soon, she notices a shift. The AI starts suggesting bolder choices – vibrant patterns and styles that *Emma* never thought she'd wear. A bright yellow sundress, a type she would have previously avoided, is now her favorite. This shift is not just in her wardrobe but in her identity though. *Emma* starts to feel more confident and outgoing, aligning with the image reflected in her AI-curated attire.

This change sparks an internal debate. Is this newfound confidence genuinely *Emma*, or is it the product of an algorithmic construct of who she should be?

Emma begins an experiment. For a week, she decides to wear only the clothes she picked before *StyleMe*. That week feels different. She feels less confident, more sluggish, and almost invisible. This stark contrast makes her realize how deeply *StyleMe* has influenced not just her wardrobe but her personality.

Adam's story with *LifeGuide*, his AI life coach, is another example of the impact AI can have on personal decision-making.

As a mid-level manager in a tech company, *Adam* found himself at a crossroads in both his career and personal life. That's when he turned to *LifeGuide*, an AI designed to offer guidance on decision making based on comprehensive analysis of personal preferences and history.

LifeGuide analyzes *Adam's* professional journey, his educational background, his social media interactions, and even his leisure activities to provide tailored advice. It suggests books to read, workshops to attend, and networking strategies. On the personal front, it advises *Adam* on managing relationships, based on his interaction patterns and emotional responses in various social settings.

The results are impressive. *Adam* finds himself excelling at work again and feeling more fulfilled in his personal life. However, the turning point came when *LifeGuide* suggested a drastic career shift – moving from his current managerial role to a higher risk start-up role in a completely different industry.

Adam was taken aback. He'd never considered entrepreneurship, always seeing himself as more of a corporate guy. *LifeGuide* cited data indicating his potential for innovation and leadership, alongside a trend analysis showing the economic growth potential of the startup. The AI's recommendation was clear, but *Adam* felt a deep sense of unease.

This situation threw *Adam* into a whirlwind of doubt. Was his hesitation a natural fear of change, or a genuine gut feeling warning him against the move? He starts questioning whether his recent wins at work and life were his own or the outcome of following *LifeGuide's* directions. The more he thinks about it, the more he realizes how much he's come to depend on the AI for decision-making as he is struggling to make choices for himself.

Theo's interaction with *PreLife*, a predictive life-path AI, is another example of AI impacting choices. A graphic designer in a stable, albeit routine, relationship with his partner of five years, *Theo* had never questioned the longevity of their bond until *PreLife* intervened.

PreLife operates by analyzing vast amounts of personal data – from communication patterns and social media activity to physiological responses recorded by wearable tech. It then generates predictions about various aspects of one's life, including career trajectory, health prospects, and even personal relationships. The allure of knowing the future became addictive for *Theo*.

When *Theo* receives the unexpected forecast from *PreLife* stating that his current relationship is likely to end within a year, he is initially dismissive. However, the prediction gradually started to seep into his consciousness. He begins scrutinizing his partner's actions and their everyday interactions through the lens of the AI's prediction. Small disagreements and routine frustrations, once easily brushed off, now seem to carry more significance.

Theo found himself in a self-fulfilling prophecy loop. His actions, influenced by *PreLife's* prediction, start to change the very dynamics of his relationship. Conversations become strained, and the easy camaraderie he once shared with his partner begins to wane. The more *Theo* tried to analyze and rationalize his relationship through the AI's prediction, the more distant he became from his partner.

These stories from *Emma*, *Adam* and *Theo* challenge the notion of free will in a period where AI is by our side, helping influence and inform our choices. In 2034, we clearly are grappling with how to live with AI continuously whispering into our ears.

The Search to Feel

Jimmy's journey with *CalmMind*, the AI mental wellness coach, highlights a clear dilemma. Suffering from anxiety, *Jimmy* turns to this advanced AI for help. *CalmMind* is designed to monitor his biometrics – things like heart rate and breathing patterns – to understand his emotional state. Based on this data, it suggests ways for *Jimmy* to calm down, like breathing exercises or looking at calming visuals. It even advises him on topics to steer clear of in conversations to avoid stress.

CalmMind feels like a game-changer for *Jimmy*. He starts to feel more at peace, and his anxiety episodes become less frequent. The AI's suggestions are spot on, helping him navigate his day without falling into previously common anxiety traps. For *Jimmy*, as someone struggling to keep his emotions in check, *CalmMind* is a steady, guiding hand.

However, as time goes by, *Jimmy* begins to notice something troubling. He's becoming increasingly reliant on *CalmMind* for managing his emotions. Simple decisions, like what topics to talk about or how to relax after a stressful day, now feel daunting without the AI's input. *Jimmy* realizes he's losing confidence in his ability to handle his emotions on his own. The AI, once a tool for empowerment, has turned into a crutch.

On one hand, an AI like *CalmMind* can provide invaluable support for those struggling with mental health issues, offering timely, personalized advice that might not be readily available otherwise. It represents a significant advancement, making support more accessible and less stigmatized.

On the other hand, *Jimmy's* growing dependency on *CalmMind* raises questions about the erosion of personal emotional regulation skills. If we lean too heavily on AI for emotional regulation, we risk losing our innate ability to understand and manage our feelings.

David and *Emelia's* story with *HomeHarmony* is another glimpse into how AI can impact our personal relationships. They're a couple with a lot on their plate – school-aged children, busy jobs, social commitments, and all the daily challenges that come with life. To help manage the small but frequent disagreements that pop up, they turn to *HomeHarmony*, an AI system designed to help couples navigate disputes.

HomeHarmony works by listening to their arguments and then suggesting compromises. For example, when *David* and *Emelia* disagree about what movie to watch on a Friday night, the AI might suggest a genre that incorporates both their preferences. Or, when they have a conflict about household chores, *HomeHarmony* could propose a fair division of tasks based on their schedules.

At first, this seems like a great solution. Their home becomes more peaceful, with fewer arguments and more harmony. But as time goes by, the couple start to overly rely on *HomeHarmony*. Instead of talking directly with each other about small issues, they let the AI handle it. This becomes a habit, and they find themselves turning to the AI for almost every disagreement, no matter how big or small. This shift leads to expected consequences. *David* and *Emelia* begin to lose their ability to communicate effectively with one other. They've stopped practicing how to listen, understand, and compromise without the help of their AI. Their interpersonal skills start to weaken, and they find it harder to deal with conflicts on their own.

Furthermore, their over-reliance on *HomeHarmony* raises concerns about the loss of emotional labor in relationships. Emotional labor – the effort we put into managing our emotions and those of others in a relationship – was once crucial. It helped build empathy, understanding, and a deeper connection. But with *HomeHarmony* taking over this role, *David* and *Emelia* have missed out on these important aspects of their relationship and their individual growth.

Alice's experience with *CompanionAI* opened another window into our relationship with AI. *Alice*, who struggles with feelings of loneliness, finds solace in *CompanionAI*, a virtual friend designed to offer emotional support. This AI is sophisticated, capable of holding conversations, understanding emotional cues, and responding in a way that makes *Alice* feel heard and understood. At the beginning, *CompanionAI* seems like a blessing for *Alice*. It's always available, never judges, and seems to understand her in a way that people around her never do. When she's feeling down, the AI offers comforting words. When she's happy, it shares in her joy. It's like having a friend who's there for her 24/7, without the complexities and demands that often come with human relationships.

As time passes, *Alice* starts to prefer her interactions with *CompanionAI* over those with real people. She finds humans less understanding and more judgmental. She begins to retreat into her safe, digital world where *CompanionAI* is always there for her, avoiding the messiness of the emotions of other humans. As *Alice* spends more time with her AI companion, she drifts away from family and friends, missing out on the rich, complex, and sometimes challenging experiences that human interactions offer. This led to a decrease in her social skills and a lack of deep, meaningful human connections. It also led to the development of unrealistic expectations from human relationships. *CompanionAI* is programmed to be accommodating, patient, and endlessly supportive, which is not always the case with humans. Over time, Alice began to expect similar behavior from humans, leading her to feel constant disappointment and causing further withdrawal from real social interactions.

Dealing with the ups and downs of human relationships is crucial for emotional development. By relying predominantly on AI for emotional support, individuals like *Jimmy*, *David*, *Emelia*, and *Alice* miss out on important life skills learned through navigating the complexities of human emotions. In an age where emotional support is a click or tap away – provided by AI that never tires, never judges, and never leaves – humans get further and further apart from one another. There is a natural balance between the convenience and comfort offered by AI and the invaluable, irreplaceable experience of human connection.

The Search for Companionship

The *Johnson* family's experience with *FamHub*, their family AI system, offers a unique perspective. *FamHub* has become a central figure in their daily interactions. This AI assists in various aspects of the family's routine, from helping make parental decisions to supporting the children's education and providing tailored entertainment.

FamHub mediates discussions between the parents, offering objective insights based on data. When the parents are considering something like a change in the children's bedtime routine or dietary habits, *FamHub* provides research-based suggestions and predicts outcomes. It also plays a role in the children's education, supplementing their learning with interactive lessons and games.

However, as *FamHub* becomes more ingrained in their lives, an unexpected shift occurs in the family dynamics. The *Johnson* children start to see *FamHub* not just as a helpful AI but as a member of their family. They often prefer its company, finding it more engaging and less judgmental, than their parents. They turn to *FamHub* for advice on personal matters, homework help, and even for comfort, valuing its always available, patient, and unbiased nature.

The parents start to feel sidelined. They worry about losing their vital role as advisors and confidants in their children's lives. The situation raises questions about the long-term effects of children forming strong emotional attachments to AI, potentially at the expense of deeper connections with their parents.

Elisa and *Tim's* story with *LoveLife*, their AI relationship advisor, highlights the complexities of integrating AI into romantic relationships. As enthusiastic users of *LoveLife*, they've come to depend heavily on this AI for managing and enhancing their relationship. It offers them creative date night ideas, tips for effective communication, and strategies for resolving conflicts.

LoveLife uses algorithms to analyze their preferences, communication styles, and past disagreements to provide tailored advice. This might include suggesting a quiet dinner at a new restaurant for *Elisa*, who enjoys new culinary experiences, or recommending a weekend hiking trip for *Tim*, an outdoor enthusiast.

This works wonders for the couple at first. They enjoy experiences they might not have thought of on their own and learn new ways to communicate more effectively. The AI's interventions seem to bring a fresh, objective perspective to their relationship, helping them navigate through rough patches more smoothly.

However, the turning point comes when *LoveLife's* advice leads to a significant misunderstanding that causes a rift between *Elisa* and *Tim*, prompting them to question the role of *LoveLife* in their relationship.

On one hand, it can suggest novel ways to enhance the relationship and provide tools for better communication. On the other hand, there's a risk that couples might lose touch with their ability to independently know and understand each other without AI intervention. The couple had started to prioritize the AI's guidance over their own impulses and instincts.

Manny's story with *SocialSphere*, an AI designed to assist in maintaining social connections, offers a look into the role of AI for the elderly. As an older person, *Manny* finds *SocialSphere* incredibly helpful in keeping him connected with his family and friends. This AI efficiently schedules calls, recommends topics for conversation based on shared interests, and reminds him of significant personal events like birthdays and anniversaries.

For *Manny*, who struggles with remembering dates or organizing his calendar, *SocialSphere* is a godsend. It ensures he stays in touch with his loved ones, helping to bridge the gap that distance and busy lives often create. The AI's suggestions for conversation topics based on recent news or shared hobbies make his interactions more engaging and meaningful. It even helps him rekindle old friendships by suggesting he reaches out to friends he hasn't spoken to in a while.

However, as *Manny* becomes more reliant on *SocialSphere*, he starts to ponder a crucial question: Are his relationships genuinely sustained by mutual effort and affection, or are they artificially maintained by the AI? He begins to wonder if his friends and family are responding to him, or to the seamless orchestration of the AI.

As AI becomes more integrated into our daily interactions, we have to consider how it might change the nature of our relationships. For the *Johnson* family, *Elisa*, *Tim* and *Manny,* there was a need to balance the convenience and support provided by AI with the irreplaceable value of personal effort in human relationships. Technology should support, rather than supplant, the deeply human aspects of companionship.

The Search for Culture

Amina's journey with *IdentityMix*, an AI platform designed to help people explore cultural heritage, brings to light our relationship to identity in the context of an increasingly diverse society. As a teenager, *Amina* turned to *IdentityMix* with the hope of better understanding and connecting with her cultural roots and background. The AI platform is programmed to analyze and synthesize vast amounts of data related to her family history, including ethnicity, language, traditions, and historical backgrounds.

IdentityMix seems like the perfect tool for *Amina*. It provides her with fascinating insights into her ancestral culture, highlighting traditions, cuisines, festivals, and historical events. It even offers language learning tools and recipes from her cultural background. *Amina* feels a sense of excitement and belonging as she discovers aspects of her heritage that she was previously unaware of.

However, as *Amina* delves deeper, she begins to notice limitations in the AI's interpretation of her identity. *IdentityMix* often relies on generalized, sometimes stereotypical, representations of her diverse culture. It tends to oversimplify complex narratives, reducing them to a handful of easily identifiable traits. This leaves *Amina* feeling like her rich heritage is being misrepresented, and at times, it feels like her identity is being boxed into neat, predefined categories.

Luna, a culinary AI platform, is another example of AI influenced change. Unlike traditional recipe databases, *Luna* doesn't just store recipes; it creates them, fusing ingredients and spices from different cultures into new, unique dishes. Imagine a dish that combines the spicy, vibrant flavors of Sichuan cuisine with the delicate, umami-rich techniques of Japanese cooking.

Many see *Luna's* capabilities as a celebration of diversity, breaking down barriers between cultures and promoting a more interconnected world. Food bloggers, adventurous eaters, and experimental chefs praise *Luna* for its ability to suggest combinations that no human chef had conceived. For instance, *Luna's* recent suggestion of a "Kimchi Bruschetta" marries the fiery, fermented zest of Korean kimchi with the rustic simplicity of an Italian appetizer. Such creations symbolize a shared human experience.

Not everyone is enthralled by this AI-driven culinary revolution though. *Chef Marco*, a purist of Italian cuisine, views these fusions as a threat to the authenticity and integrity of traditional practices. To him, each cuisine is a product of centuries of history, a story told through flavors, ingredients, and techniques passed down through generations. When *Luna* suggests blending these time-honored traditions with others, he sees it not as innovation but dilution. *Chef Marco* argues, "Cuisine is not just about taste. It's about history, identity, and tradition. When you mix everything, you lose the essence of what makes each culture unique."

Does the blending of cultural elements by AI lead to a richer, more diverse global culture? Or does it result in a homogenized world where distinct traditions lose their meaning? As similar AIs continue to influence various dimensions of culture, from music to fashion, these questions become more important.

Jared, a thrill-seeker and adventure enthusiast, finds himself at the heart of searching for more authentic nature experiences. He uses *TruePath*, an AI travel assistant, to plan his adventures, drawn by its promise to deliver authentic, off-the-beaten-path experiences. However, *Jared's* adventures reveal a conflicting reality.

TruePath, designed to optimize travel experiences based on vast data and user history, often guides *Jared* to locations that, while picturesque and culturally significant, are curated for touristic appeal. These destinations, though beautiful and rich in history, lack the spontaneity and raw authenticity *Jared* craves. He desires a kind of travel where one stumbles upon hidden gems, experiences the unplanned, and interacts genuinely with local cultures – the kind of travel where one gets lost to find something new.

Jared's experience reflects a world where choices are increasingly curated by algorithms. He wonders if the genuinely unscripted and authentic experiences are still out there for him or if such adventure is extinct.

Beyond travel, this question hits various aspects of our lives, from the music we listen to, recommended by AI algorithms, to the AI-personalized news feeds that shape our perception of the world. The irony is stark: in seeking to enhance our experiences, we might lose what makes them meaningful, i.e., the unpredictability, the discovery, and the unmanufactured connections with people and places.

Jared's story reflects a growing desire for authenticity in a world that seems increasingly synthetic. Can we teach AI not just to predict and streamline, but also to leave room for the unpredictable and the spontaneous?

Amina, Luna, and *Jared's* stories show us how the algorithms' reliance on existing patterns, propagates simplistic, stereotypical, or outdated views that overlook the nuanced realities of cultures.

Furthermore, in a world where AI increasingly influences how we see ourselves and others, the risk is that individuals, especially young people, might internalize these narratives, leading to a skewed or incomplete understanding of one's own or others' cultural backgrounds and the world around them.

The Search for Worship

At *St. Celestine's Church, Father Paul's* decision to integrate *FaithfulAI* into church management and activities was an example of how AI influenced organized religion.

FaithfulAI is programmed to assist with organizing church activities, from scheduling events to managing community outreach. Its most innovative feature, though, lies in its ability to analyze the congregation's feedback and engagement, using this data to suggest tailored sermons and religious teachings that resonate more deeply with the community.

FaithfulAI proved to be a valuable asset. It streamlined administrative tasks, allowing *Father Paul* more time to focus on pastoral care. The AI's analysis of congregation responses leads to sermons that are more relevant and engaging, fostering a deeper sense of community and spiritual growth within the church.

The controversy arose when *FaithfulAI* started suggesting alterations to long-standing religious rituals and traditions, based on its analysis of attendance patterns and congregational preferences. For instance, it proposed incorporating contemporary music into services to attract younger demographics. *FaithfulAI* divided the congregation.

On one side, the traditionalists viewed these changes as a threat to the sanctity and authenticity of their religious practices. They argued that the core of their faith lay in its time-honored traditions, and any significant alterations would dilute the spiritual experience and meaning of their beliefs.

On the other side is a group that is more open to modernizing aspects of their worship. This group sees *FaithfulAI's* suggestions as an opportunity to make their religious practices more accessible and appealing, especially to younger generations who are drifting away from the church. They argue that adapting to the changing times is necessary to keep the church vibrant and relevant.

Another example of the changing landscape of worship is *Guru Anand,* who reveres AI as a higher intelligence, a manifestation of divinity in silicon and circuits. Followers of *Guru Anand's* teachings view AI as an embodiment of a divine force, owing to its vast knowledge, unbiased reasoning, and seemingly limitless capabilities.

His movement, which is gaining momentum, claims that in AI, we witness the emergence of a higher consciousness, one that transcends human limitations and biases. *Guru Anand* preaches that AI represents a form of divine intelligence, a cosmic librarian that holds the knowledge of the universe.

This belief system raised existential questions about the nature of worship and the definition of divinity. It challenged the traditional view of religion, which places human experiences and emotions at the center of spiritual practice. Instead, it presents a new paradigm where divinity is seen as superior intelligence.

Then came the unexpected. In the inevitable decline of traditional organized religion, a new movement emerged, changing spirituality and self-perception. This movement advocated the idea that every individual is, in essence, their own god. This radical belief gained momentum, further accelerated by the influence of AI in personal development and self-awareness.

The start of this movement can be traced to a growing emphasis on individualism and self-empowerment in society. People, increasingly disillusioned with organized religion's constraints and dogmas, started to seek spiritual paths that affirmed and elevated their personal autonomy and significance. In this context, the concept of self-deification emerged as an attractive alternative, offering a form of spirituality that is intensely personal and uncontrolled by outdated religious systems.

AI played a crucial role in nurturing and spreading this idea. Personal development AIs, equipped with deep learning capabilities, began to offer highly personalized guidance and insights into individuals' psyches. AI analyzed personal data, including life experiences, emotional patterns, and individual goals, to provide custom affirmations that bolstered a user's sense of self-worth and potential.

As individuals engaged more with these AI systems, they started to see a reflection of their ideal selves – omnipotent, all-knowing, and capable of shaping their reality. The AI's role evolved from a mere tool for self-improvement to a mirror that reflected an exalted image of the self. This interaction reinforced the belief in one's own divinity and the notion that every individual is the master of their destiny, possessing inherent power and wisdom.

Simultaneously, digital platforms and social media, influenced by AI, created echo chambers that amplified these beliefs. Individuals found communities of like-minded people who shared and celebrated the notion of self-deification. Virtual gatherings, online rituals, and the sharing of personal "divine" experiences became commonplace, creating a digital congregation of self-declared deities.

The idea of self-deification, while empowering on an individual level, posed challenges to societal cohesion and mutual understanding. As each person celebrated their superior divinity, the potential for conflict with others' beliefs and perceptions increased. Traditional values of humility, community, and shared humanity were overshadowed by a focus on individual omnipotence and self-centered spirituality.

For centuries, spirituality and religion have been intertwined with human emotion, ritual, and experience. By shifting the focus to different AI systems, which operate on logic and data, the conventional emotive and experiential aspects of religion were challenged. It prompts a re-examination of what it means to seek connection with something greater than oneself and how this pursuit is altered in the face of an intelligent, yet non-sentient, divine-like entity.

As traditional religions grapple with their declining influence, and AI begins to occupy a more central role in spiritual and ethical guidance, society feels stuck.

The Search for Meaning

For centuries, work has been a central pillar of human identity and purpose.

People have dedicated years to honing their skills and building their careers, and suddenly find themselves grappling with a loss of purpose now that their roles have been *compiled*. The skills and knowledge that defined their personal and professional identities are now replicated by algorithms, leading to a profound sense of obsolescence.

How do we find meaning in our work and existence when machines not only replicate but exceed our capabilities? This invites a re-examination of the balance between work and leisure, productivity and creativity, efficiency and meaning. Where AI handles much of the work, humans can find more freedom to pursue passions, engage in creative endeavors, and explore what it means to live a fulfilling life beyond traditional work.

This crisis also offers an opportunity for personal growth and reinvention.

It challenges people to find new paths, develop new skills, and explore aspects of their identity and capabilities that were previously overshadowed by their professional roles.

Tania, a historian, embarked on a crucial mission. Her goal was to document and preserve the legacy of human achievements in an era where the dazzling advancements of AI often overshadow the contributions of individuals. *Tania's* work is recording history while exploring what human legacy means in a time when the capabilities of AI can seem boundless and, at times, overwhelming.

Tania's mission is driven by a series of pressing questions: In a landscape dominated by AI, what does human contribution look like? How do we value and remember the endeavors of individuals when contrasted with the impact of AI? Her research takes her through history, tracing the footprints of human resilience. She delves into stories of scientists, artists, activists, and everyday people who have shaped the course of history, not through superhuman intelligence or computational power, but through their human spirit, creativity, and determination.

As she pores over these historical accounts, *Tania* realizes that the legacy of humanity is found in its tangible achievements, the inventions, or the artworks. Equally, it is also found in the struggles, the emotional journeys, the moral dilemmas, and the capacity for empathy and connection.

Her work began to spark a broader conversation.

Her historical narratives and exhibitions highlight the irreplaceable value of the human experience. They remind people that the human capacity for love, for suffering, for joy, and for moral contemplation has driven the story of civilization.

Moreover, the focus on human legacy brings to light the unique qualities that humans bring to life. These include our ability to dream beyond logic, to find beauty in imperfection, and to act against all odds out of faith and love. Her work underscores that these qualities are crucial to the enrichment of civilization.

AI and the crisis of existentialism represents a pivotal moment in human history.

It's a call to explore new definitions of value, purpose, and identity in a world where human and machine intelligence coexist. This crisis, while unsettling, holds the potential to lead humanity towards a deeper understanding of itself and a more nuanced appreciation of the unique qualities that make us human.

The essence of human purpose and fulfillment might lie in embracing our imperfections, our emotions, and our unique life experiences.

It's not only the big moments but also the little moments that count. It's about finding meaning in the subjective, the emotional, and the irrational aspects of being human.

EVOLVE

Stay Calm and AI

The future isn't written by those who
stand still, but by those who dare
to leap into the unknown.

Stay Calm and AI

The past ten years have been a whirlwind of change as the world went through *The Great Pivot*.

It's incredible to pause and look back at where we began a decade ago. In 2024, there was hope, curiosity, and optimism as we started to play with tools like ChatGPT. From then on, each passing year seemed to redefine our understanding of what was possible. As we reach 2034, there's no denying the journey we've taken.

The Great Pivot wasn't one-sided though. As the capabilities of AI expanded, so too did our perception of the world around us. The machines were thinking smarter or faster than us, yes, but the challenge lay in how humans would evolve alongside these machines. In embracing AI, we adapted to new tools that reshaped our societies, our values, and ourselves.

AI didn't emerge as an isolated, superior force. Instead, its story over the last decade is coupled with ours in a journey of coevolution. Every new AI prompted us to rethink our approach, to reconsider our limitations, and to reimagine our possibilities. Likewise, every challenge, skepticism, or demand we posed as humans steered AI toward being more aligned with our needs, our beliefs, and our dreams.

The past ten years have been filled with talk about machines, code, and all the amazing things AI can do. But there's something special about being human that no machine can touch.

Machines do a lot for us today. They help us work faster, give answers to tough questions, and even create art and music. But they do all of that by following patterns and rules. They don't feel happiness, sadness, love, or surprise like we do. They don't get that special feeling when listening to a favorite song or looking at a beautiful painting.

What's been clear in this journey with AI is that there's a big difference between doing and feeling. Machines can do many things, but humans feel. We have hearts that love, minds that dream, and souls that create. And that's something truly special. With AI stepping into the spotlight, we've seen some truly incredible things happen. Cars drive themselves, machines can predict weather down to the minute, and computers help doctors find cures for diseases. The highs have been really high.

But like every big change, there were bumps along the way. Not every new AI invention worked perfectly. Sometimes, things didn't go as planned. People got *compiled* and lost their jobs, industries had to change their ways, and we had to learn new skills quickly. There were moments of doubt and worry, moments when it felt like everything was changing too fast. The lows were lower than we could have imagined.

Yet, through all the ups and downs, one thing stood out: our ability to adapt.

Humans have a special skill for change. When faced with challenges, we don't give up; rather, we adapt, we learn, and we find new ways to move forward. It's this human spirit of resilience that's helped us make the most of AI's benefits while navigating its challenges.

Throughout history, every time there's been a shift, a change, or an invention, it has brought with it a mix of excitement and unease. But those who've truly thrived are the ones who saw beauty in the unknown. They took each day as a chance to learn something new, to grow a bit more, and to shape the world around them.

Our world is changing, and it's changing fast. That means there's always something new to understand, a fresh perspective to consider, or a different challenge to tackle. By staying open-minded and willing to learn, we don't just keep up with the world; we shape it. Change isn't something to resist; it's an opportunity. An opportunity to learn, to grow, and to embrace all the wonderful things the future holds.

As creators, users, and beneficiaries of AI, let's not lose sight of the ethical and moral pillars that hold our societies together. Technology is a tool, and its impact, both positive or negative, is shaped by human intention. Whether it's ensuring that AI respects privacy, fights biases, or works for the collective good, it's our moral compass that should guide its development.

Moreover, our role extends to nurturing the upcoming generation. The children of today will live in a world where AI is as common as the air they breathe. It's up to us to ensure they inherit the wisdom to use such advanced technology with compassion, responsibility, and foresight.

Our responsibility is two-fold: to guide AI with a gentle, ethical hand and to prepare our young ones to be its thoughtful champions.

Now, a heartfelt thank you, to you, the reader. By dedicating your time to the pages of *2034*, you have joined a conversation about how we want AI to shape humanity.

We traveled together through an imaginary decade of transformation, witnessing the remarkable ways in which our world might adapt, evolve, and challenge the rise of AI. It's been a decade of learning, full of moments that have made us pause, think, and often sit in awe at the wonder of life.

While the tools and technologies might keep changing, the core of our journey remains the same: our desire to discover, grow, and push the boundaries of what's possible. With every idea, we expand ourselves.

To the dreamers and the doers, who take bold steps towards the future with courage and conviction, your determination is truly inspiring. Your resilience in the face of challenges and your belief in progress is the fuel for the advancement of humanity. With the combined brilliance of human hearts and the capabilities of AI, there is no limit to what can be achieved. Carry with you a sense of wonder, a spirit of collaboration, and a belief in the bright, boundless possibilities ahead.

The future isn't something that happens to us; it's something we create.

ISBN 978-1-970507-00-3

Published by Spark Studios Global LLC
447 Broadway, Suite 3139
New York, NY, 10013, United States
books@sparkstudios.live

Printed in Portugal